vivafood

Penguin Group

02acknowledgements

The recipes in *viva food* have been selected from my weekly column in *viva*, part of the *New Zealand Herald* on Wednesdays. I give grateful thanks to all the people who have helped bring this book to fruition.

Special thanks go to talented *viva* photographer Carolyn Robertson, for capturing my food so delightfully with your eye for perfection and your camera. It has been an absolute pleasure to work with you over the past four seasons. Thank you Michele Crawshaw, editor of *viva*, for your excellent editorial assistance and for fostering this project. My thanks go to you and the *viva* team for supporting me as food editor with your dedicated work throughout the year.

Many thanks go to Bernice Beachman, my publisher at Penguin Books (NZ), for this brilliant idea and for your year-round support. Thank you Philippa Gerrard, my editor at Penguin, for your kindness, sensitive editing and thoroughness in production. And thank you Athena Sommerfeld, for expertly weaving everything together into a beautiful design.

Thank you Fiona Barber for lending your lovely composed hands to some of these images – and thanks Sophia for being such a little angel.

PENGUIN BOOKS
Published by the Penguin Group
Penguin Group (NZ), cnr Airborne and Rosedale Roads, Albany,
Auckland 1310, New Zealand (a division of Pearson New Zealand Ltd)
Penguin Group (USA) Inc., 375 Hudson Street,
New York, New York 10014, USA
Penguin Group (Canada), 10 Alcorn Avenue, Toronto,
Ontario, Canada M4V 3B2 (a division of Pearson Penguin Canada Inc.)
Penguin Books Ltd, 80 Strand, London, WC2R 0RL, England
Penguin Ireland, 25 St Stephen's Green,
Dublin 2, Ireland (a division of Penguin Books Ltd)
Penguin Group (Australia), 250 Camberwell Road, Camberwell,
Victoria 3124, Australia (a division of Pearson Australia Group Pty Ltd)
Penguin Books India Pvt Ltd, 11, Community Centre,
Panchsheel Park, New Delhi - 110 017, India
Penguin Books (South Africa) (Pty) Ltd, 24 Sturdee Avenue,
Rosebank, Johannesburg 2196, South Africa

Penguin Books Ltd, Registered Offices: 80 Strand, London, WC2R 0RL, England

First published by Penguin Group (NZ), 2005
1 3 5 7 9 10 8 6 4 2

Copyright © recipes Julie Le Clerc, 2005
Copyright © photographs New Zealand Herald, 2005

The right of Julie Le Clerc to be identified as the author of this work
in terms of section 96 of the Copyright Act 1994 is hereby asserted.

Designed and typeset by Athena Sommerfeld
Prepress by microdot
Printed in China through Bookbuilders, Hong Kong

ISBN 0 14 302032 3
A catalogue record for this book is available from the National Library of New Zealand.

www.penguin.co.nz

vivafood

FOUR SEASONS OF SENSATIONAL FLAVOURS

viva.
The New Zealand Herald

Julie Le Clerc

photography Carolyn Robertson

contents

The ever-changing seasons provide a revolving array of fresh ingredients that tantalise the taste-buds and stimulate the minds of good cooks. With this collection of recipes, I invite you to explore the particular essential flavours of each distinct season and to take pleasure in cooking and sharing dishes that capture this naturally occurring variety and profusion.

Fruits and vegetables that have been allowed to properly ripen in their rightful season are bursting with colour, perfume, taste and texture. Picked at the peak of perfection, fresh, locally grown crops hold greater nutritional value than any cool-store counterparts, which never truly reach their full potential. And, as an added bonus, because food grown in-season is plentiful, this naturally occurring over-supply causes prices to plummet – meaning that shopping for excellent produce can be relatively inexpensive.

I use fresh seasonal produce as a constant source of inspiration for my home cooking. I'll take what is plentiful in the market and use this to determine what I cook on any particular day. I recommend you do the same – buy whatever catches your eye and substitute this for something else in a recipe you fancy. In this way, you will find that different times of year will stimulate a different inclination to create enticing dishes that naturally fit each season.

The beauty of incorporating luscious seasonal ingredients in cooking is that they give every particle of flavour they have to the dish. Produce grown in its natural season is full of genuine flavour. It tastes intensely real. It stands to reason therefore that if you shop well for quality produce, handle it with care, and cook in an honest and passionate way, then the result will be powerful flavours.

One of the joys of cooking and eating such good food is that it creates indelible taste memories. Perhaps this is why we long for the deeply flavoured strawberries of our youth. Or, why we can vividly remember food eaten on holiday in countries that still respect seasonal cooking, such as Italy, France, Greece and Spain (to name but a few).

I like to shop for food most days, as they do in Europe, buying little and often to guarantee freshness and gain full nutritional value. If you choose to make freshness and flavour a priority, then it's possible to build this shopping into your day too. Initially, searching for quality may take a little extra time until you get to know what's in, where and when – though you can spot such produce easily because it will be displayed in luscious, bountiful piles.

Use your senses to help determine what's good at any time. I will smell, touch, inspect and taste, if possible, before I buy any produce because the rewards of obtaining the best available ingredients are gratifying, especially when friends and family benefit from my labours.

Other ways of finding current seasonal produce, and having fun at the same time, include taking a drive in the countryside to shop at rural roadside stalls, fruit-sheds, and pick-your-own farms. Farmers' markets, which are happily multiplying, sell a plethora of just-harvested, farm-fresh produce and sometimes wonderful heirloom varieties that retain the flavours of the past. When I think, for example, of the unforced, gigantic, sun-warmed, fragrant, redder-than-red beefsteak tomatoes that my father grows in his own garden, my mouth waters in anticipation of summer.

Each returning season brings with it particular tastes and pleasures. The long, warm days of summer highlight orchards, fields and market gardens overflowing with sun-ripened berries, stone fruits, tomatoes, salad leaves, flowers and honey-bees. Seafood sparkles fresh from the sea. And summertime brings with it the glorious opportunity for cooking and eating outdoors.

The delights of autumn are displayed in a rustic harvest of mushrooms, nuts, pumpkins and squash, apples and pears, plus some special gifts that make only a brief appearance at this time, such as figs and quince. Winter is a season when we can relish nature's robust flavours in home-made pies, nourishing soups, slow-cooked stews, and comforting sticky puddings that warm us from the inside.

And with the start of spring, when the first tender asparagus appears, we can celebrate by cooking recipes that take advantage of renewed freshness and light.

This book represents a year of seasonal cooking. Because what we eat matters, these recipes are full of naturally fresh, seasonal ingredients. While some ingredients overlap different seasons, and others may be available all year round, I have placed each one according to the season when they are at their best.

If you choose to cook with the rhythm of the seasons, you will be generously rewarded with food full of lively, pure and natural flavours. I believe that stylishly simple, tasty recipes are the best way to exploit such abundance. The following seasonal dishes allow each special ingredient to shine in its own right, or gently meld in harmony with other tastes. It is my hope that you will bring these recipes home to your own kitchen, cook them with love, and enjoy feasting in season.

Julie Le Clerc

08 summer

SUMMER DAZZLES US WITH SPARKLING SEAFOOD
AND FRESH PRODUCE FULL OF VIBRANT COLOURS
AND LIGHT, CLEAN, FRAGRANT TASTES. SUMMER FOOD
SINGS WITH SIMPLICITY AND FRESHNESS. HOT, SUNNY
DAYS PROVIDE A CHANCE TO ENJOY BARBECUES AND
PICNICS – A TIME TO COMPOSE UNCOMPLICATED
MEALS THAT REVITALISE THE SENSES.

MIXED TOMATO SALAD WITH PROSCIUTTO DRESSING

Oven drying tomatoes concentrates their intensity of flavour. These semi-dried tomato halves are wonderful in salads or they can be served as a snack or as part of antipasti.

12 SMALL ROMA TOMATOES, HALVED

OLIVE OIL

SEA SALT AND FRESHLY GROUND
BLACK PEPPER

1 PUNNET RED OR YELLOW
CHERRY TOMATOES

1/2 CUP QUALITY SUN-DRIED TOMATOES

1/4 CUP TORN BASIL LEAVES

1 Preheat oven to 120°C. Place roma tomato halves on a lightly oiled baking tray, cut-side up, drizzle with a little olive oil and season with salt and pepper. Bake for 1½–2 hours until semi-dried. Remove to cool.

2 Place all the different types of tomatoes with the basil leaves in a large bowl.

3 Combine chopped prosciutto, garlic, balsamic vinegar and olive oil to form a dressing and season with salt and pepper to taste. Pour dressing over tomato salad and toss well.

serves 4–6

PROSCIUTTO DRESSING

6 SLICES PROSCIUTTO, ROUGHLY CHOPPED

2 CLOVES GARLIC, CRUSHED

2 TABLESPOONS BALSAMIC VINEGAR

3 TABLESPOONS EXTRA VIRGIN OLIVE OIL

GOOD IDEA ...
TO STORE SEMI-DRIED TOMATOES, DRIZZLE WITH
A LITTLE BALSAMIC VINEGAR AND PACK INTO A
CLEAN JAR. COVER TOMATOES WITH QUALITY EXTRA
VIRGIN OLIVE OIL, THEN SEAL THE JAR. SEMI-DRIED
TOMATOES WILL LAST FOR UP TO TWO WEEKS
STORED IN THE FRIDGE. SERVE IN SALADS OR AS
AN ANTIPASTO.

CHILLI-ROASTED CORN WHEELS

Alternatively, these wheels of sweetcorn can be barbecued or char-grilled, which gives a smoky flavour to the kernels. Serve this interesting rendition hot as a vegetable dish or cold as a salad.

5–6 COBS FRESH SWEETCORN

¼ CUP OLIVE OIL

2 CLOVES GARLIC, CRUSHED

1 TEASPOON CHILLI FLAKES

SEA SALT AND FRESHLY GROUND
BLACK PEPPER

3 TABLESPOONS CHOPPED FRESH
CORIANDER, OR PARSLEY IF PREFERRED

1 Heat oven to 200°C. Chop sweetcorn cobs into 2cm thick rounds and place in an oven pan. Drizzle with olive oil and scatter with garlic, chilli flakes, salt and pepper. Toss well to evenly coat wheels of corn.

2 Place in oven and roast for 15 minutes or until golden brown, tossing once during cooking.

3 Remove from the oven and sprinkle with chopped coriander or parsley.

serves 6 as a side dish

SHORTCUT …
WHEN HARVESTED, CORN COMES WRAPPED IN A
NATURAL HUSK AND CAN BE BAKED OR BARBECUED
WHOLE SO THAT THE CORN STEAMS WITHIN THIS
PROTECTIVE CASING. TO STEAM OR BOIL CORN,
SIMPLY STRIP OFF THE HUSK AND SILKY THREADS
AND COOK FOR 5 MINUTES BEFORE SEASONING
AND SMEARING WITH BUTTER OR DRIZZLING WITH
EXTRA VIRGIN OLIVE OIL.

SHAVED CORN & PRAWN SALAD WITH CORN & DILL AIOLI

I have made a corn and dill aioli for this corn and prawn salad because its creaminess complements the crispness of the salad. If you prefer something less rich, maybe opt for a fresh salsa of corn kernels with dill, chilli, diced tomatoes and red onion.

20 KING PRAWNS, HEADS AND SHELLS REMOVED LEAVING TAILS INTACT

2 COBS FRESH SWEETCORN

1 RED ONION, FINELY SLICED

½ CUP QUALITY SUN-DRIED TOMATOES, HALVED

1 COS LETTUCE, LEAVES SEPARATED AND WASHED

1 Place 3cm of water in a large saucepan and bring to the boil. Add the prawns and turn off the heat. Remove prawns after 2–3 minutes or when they have turned a deep pinky-orange and are just cooked through. Set aside to cool.

2 With a sharp knife, remove and discard the dark veins running down the back of each prawn.

3 Steam or boil sweetcorn for 5 minutes, drain and cool. Once cold, remove kernels by shaving cobs with a sharp knife.

4 Combine cold prawns and corn kernels with remaining salad ingredients in a bowl. Serve with corn and dill aioli on the side.

CORN & DILL AIOLI

2 EGG YOLKS

JUICE OF 1 LEMON

SEA SALT

3 CLOVES GARLIC, PEELED

½ CUP RAW SWEETCORN KERNELS, REMOVED FROM THE COB

1 TABLESPOON CHOPPED FRESH DILL

½ CUP MILD-FLAVOURED OLIVE OIL

1 Place egg yolks and lemon juice in the bowl of a food processor with a little salt and process until pale and fluffy.

2 Add the garlic, sweetcorn kernels and chopped dill to the bowl. With the motor running, slowly drizzle in olive oil until amalgamated and the mixture is thick and creamy.

serves 4

MY ADVICE ...
AIM TO COOK CORN SOON AFTER PURCHASE WHEN IT'S AT ITS FRESHEST – AND DON'T SALT THE WATER BEFORE COOKING AS SALT INHIBITS THE SOFTENING OF THE KERNELS.

MY ADVICE …
WHEN BARBECUING, BROWN FOOD
FIRST OVER THE HOTTEST PART OF THE
BARBECUE, THEN TO FINISH COOKING
WITHOUT BURNING, TRANSFER FOOD
TO A PART OF THE BARBECUE WHERE
THE HEAT IS LESS FIERCE (OR TURN
DOWN THE HEAT).

POUSSINS MARINATED IN LEMON & MARJORAM

It is worth taking the time to marinate foods, as a good marinade adds flavour, tenderises meat, and when used to baste foods during cooking will help stop them drying out.

4 SMALL POUSSINS (BABY CHICKENS)

1/4 CUP OLIVE OIL

FINELY GRATED ZEST AND JUICE OF 2 LEMONS

2 CLOVES GARLIC, CRUSHED

3 TABLESPOONS ROUGHLY CHOPPED FRESH MARJORAM (OR OREGANO)

SEA SALT AND FRESHLY GROUND BLACK PEPPER

EXTRA LEMONS, HALVED TO GARNISH

1 With kitchen scissors or a sharp knife, cut down either side of the backbone of each poussin; discard the backbones. Flatten the poussins by placing each on a board and pressing down firmly on the breast. Cut each poussin in half and secure in a flat position by skewering with stainless-steel skewers.

2 Place poussins in a deep sided ceramic dish. Cover with olive oil, lemon zest and juice, garlic, and marjoram. Leave to marinate for several hours or overnight, turning once or twice during this time so that the meat marinates evenly.

3 Remove poussins from marinade, dry with paper towels and season with salt and pepper. Cook on a preheated barbecue for 10–15 minutes on each side, basting occasionally with marinade until cooked – this is when the juices run clear after a sharp knife is inserted deep into the leg joint.

4 At the same time barbecue the lemon halves to serve as a garnish.

serves 4

BARBECUE TERIYAKI SALMON

Cooking over coals makes food taste great. For me, the beautiful smoky, juicy barbecue flavours are a happy reminder of growing up.

3CM PIECE FRESH GINGER, PEELED AND ROUGHLY CHOPPED
1/2 CUP LIGHT SOY SAUCE
1/2 CUP MIRIN (JAPANESE SWEET RICE WINE), OR SUBSTITUTE SWEET SHERRY
JUICE OF 2 LIMES
800G SIDE OF FRESH SALMON, WITH THE SKIN ON
LIME WEDGES TO GARNISH

1 Place ginger, soy sauce, mirin and lime juice in a saucepan. Bring to the boil, simmer for 2 minutes for flavours to infuse, then strain, discard ginger and set liquid aside to cool.

2 Remove pin bones from salmon with tweezers, or get your fishmonger to do this for you. Slice salmon into 4 equal portions. Place salmon, skin-side up, in a flat, non-metallic dish to fit snugly. Pour over cold marinade, cover and refrigerate for 2 hours.

3 Drain salmon and cook on a preheated barbecue for about 2 minutes on each side for medium-rare (cook a little longer if your preference is for well-done). Serve with lime wedges to squeeze over.

serves 4

MY ADVICE …
WHEN BARBECUING, DON'T COOK OVER A DIRECT FLAME, AS FOOD WILL BURN TO A CRISP BEFORE COOKING THROUGH. WAIT UNTIL THE FLAMES HAVE DIED DOWN OR RAISE FOOD AWAY FROM THE FLAMES.

GAZPACHO

I've added a little Spanish smoked paprika to my favourite gazpacho for extra piquancy. This soup sparkles with flavour – sipped on a hot summer's day, it is wonderfully refreshing.

2 SLICES STALE WHOLEGRAIN BREAD, CRUSTS REMOVED

½ CUP COLD WATER

2 CLOVES GARLIC, CRUSHED

6 LARGE RIPE TOMATOES, PEELED AND SEEDS REMOVED

½ TELEGRAPH CUCUMBER, PEELED, SEEDS REMOVED, ROUGHLY CHOPPED

1 RED PEPPER, SEEDS REMOVED, ROUGHLY CHOPPED

1 RED ONION, FINELY CHOPPED

1 TEASPOON SUGAR

3 TABLESPOONS SHERRY OR RED WINE VINEGAR

4 TABLESPOONS EXTRA VIRGIN OLIVE OIL

1 TEASPOON SWEET SMOKED SPANISH PAPRIKA

SEA SALT AND FRESHLY GROUND BLACK PEPPER

ICE CUBES TO SERVE

1 Place bread in a bowl, pour over cold water and set aside to soften for 5–10 minutes. Meanwhile, prepare the vegetables, reserving a quarter cup of each to finely dice and serve as a garnish.

2 Blend wet bread with remaining ingredients, except salt, pepper and ice cubes, in a blender. Purée in two batches if necessary and adjust seasoning at end of processing.

3 Cover and refrigerate until cold or preferably overnight to allow flavours to develop. When ready to serve, place a few ice cubes into each bowl or glass, pour on gazpacho and garnish with finely diced tomato, cucumber, pepper and red onion.

serves 4

GRILLED CHICKEN WITH AVOCADO & CHILLI SALSA

To achieve attractive crosshatch grill marks on food, cook chicken breasts for 4 minutes on the barbecue or char-grill pan, then give the chicken a quarter turn and continue cooking.

4 SKINLESS CHICKEN BREASTS

1 TABLESPOON AVOCADO OR OLIVE OIL

SEA SALT AND FRESHLY GROUND BLACK PEPPER

AVOCADO & CHILLI SALSA

2 AVOCADOS, PEELED AND STONES REMOVED

1 RED CHILLI, SEEDS REMOVED, CHOPPED

4 SPRING ONIONS, FINELY SLICED

1/4 CUP CHOPPED FRESH CORIANDER

FINELY GRATED ZEST AND JUICE OF 3 LIMES

2 TABLESPOONS AVOCADO OR OLIVE OIL

SEA SALT AND FRESHLY GROUND BLACK PEPPER

1 Brush the chicken breasts with a little avocado oil and season with salt and pepper. Either char-grill, barbecue, grill or fry chicken in a non-stick frying pan over a medium heat for 8–10 minutes on each side or until cooked through.

2 Meanwhile, dice the avocado flesh and combine in a bowl with the remaining salsa ingredients. Season with salt and pepper and toss well.

3 Serve generous amounts of salsa over the cooked chicken breasts. Accompany with plenty of steamed greens on the side.

serves 4

MY ADVICE ...
CHOOSE TO USE QUALITY OLIVE OIL OR AVOCADO OIL IN COOKING. NOT ONLY DO THESE GOOD OILS HAVE WONDERFUL FLAVOUR, BUT THEY HOLD MANY HEALTH BENEFITS TOO. THEY'RE RICH IN MONO-UNSATURATED FATS (THE GOOD GUYS), WHICH HELP REDUCE THE BAD AND ENCOURAGE THE GOOD CHOLESTEROL IN OUR BLOOD. PLUS THEY CONTAIN NATURAL ANTIOXIDANTS THAT ASSIST IN PROTECTING US AGAINST ILLNESS.

MEDITERRANEAN VEGETABLE PIES

This vegetable filling can be prepared in advance – and the same goes for the pastry cases, then simply assemble the pies when needed. I also recommend serving these pies with a dollop of basil pesto on top. Try making your own, as home-made pesto has superior flavour – for a recipe see page 127.

PASTRY

150G BUTTER, CUBED
2 CUPS PLAIN FLOUR
¼ TEASPOON SEA SALT
3 TABLESPOONS COLD WATER

FILLING

300G (1 MEDIUM) EGGPLANT, CUT INTO LARGE CUBES
2 RED PEPPERS, SEEDS REMOVED, SLICED
3 MEDIUM COURGETTES, THICKLY SLICED
150G BUTTON MUSHROOMS, HALVED
¼ CUP OLIVE OIL
SEA SALT AND FRESHLY GROUND BLACK PEPPER
2 TABLESPOONS CHOPPED FRESH OREGANO

1 Rub butter into flour by hand or in a food processor until the mixture resembles breadcrumbs. Mix in salt, then the cold water until dough comes together in a ball. Cover pastry with plastic wrap and refrigerate to rest for 30 minutes.

2 Preheat oven to 200°C. Place eggplant, peppers, courgettes and mushrooms in a large oven pan. Drizzle with olive oil; season with salt and pepper and toss well. Roast for 30 minutes or until golden brown and tender, tossing once during cooking. Remove to cool.

3 Roll out pastry to 4mm thick and use to line 8 x 10cm pie tins. Trim edges and prick bases with a fork. Chill for 30 minutes. Line pastry cases with foil and fill with baking beans to bake blind for 15 minutes at 180°C. Remove baking beans and foil and return pastry cases to the oven for a further 5 minutes until dry and crisp. At this stage pastry cases can be frozen for a later date (see note).

4 When required, fill pastry cases with roast vegetables and garnish with oregano.

makes 8

GOOD IDEA …
MAKE A BIG BATCH OF PASTRY CASES AND FREEZE THE EXCESS IN A CONTAINER FOR UP TO TWO MONTHS. WHEN YOU ARE READY, THAW THE CASES AS NEEDED BEFORE FILLING WITH THE ROASTED MEDITERRANEAN VEGETABLES. TO FRESHEN THAWED PIE CASES, BAKE FOR 5 MINUTES IN A HOT OVEN.

TUNA & CRISPY NOODLE SALAD

The wonderful combination of textures in this salad makes for an intriguing taste sensation. Substitute sliced roast chicken, crispy grilled bacon, shaved ham or any seafood you fancy for the canned tuna, if desired.

375G CAN TUNA IN SPRING WATER, DRAINED AND FLAKED

¼ CHINESE CABBAGE, FINELY SHREDDED

140G PACKET CRISPY NOODLES

1 SMALL RED ONION, FINELY SLICED

1 LARGE CARROT, PEELED AND CUT INTO VERY FINE STRIPS

1 RED PEPPER, SEEDS REMOVED, FINELY SLICED

1 CUP MUNG BEAN SPROUTS

3 TABLESPOONS CHOPPED FRESH CORIANDER OR PARSLEY

1 Combine prepared salad ingredients in a large bowl.

2 Mix dressing ingredients together, adjusting proportions as necessary, to achieve a balanced sweet-sour-hot-salty flavour. Pour dressing over salad and toss well.

serves 4

LIME & CHILLI DRESSING

3–4 TABLESPOONS SWEET CHILLI SAUCE

JUICE OF 3–4 LIMES

1–2 TABLESPOONS LIGHT SOY SAUCE

3 TABLESPOONS PEANUT OR SUNFLOWER OIL

SERVING SUGGESTION ...
FOR A PERFECT MATCH, SERVE THE
SAME WINE AT THE TABLE AS YOU USED
IN COOKING THIS DISH. PERHAPS TRY
THE SNAPPER AND CHARDONNAY PIES
FOR SUNDAY LUNCH, SERVED WITH A
LOVELY BUTTERY CHARDONNAY.

SNAPPER & CHARDONNAY PIES

Heavy oak flavour can be a problem in reds as well as white wines used in cooking, so add these with care or they can overpower the other ingredients. For example, in the following dish it is best to opt for an unoaked chardonnay as the cooking process will concentrate any strong oaky flavours.

3 TABLESPOONS OLIVE OIL

1 ONION, FINELY CHOPPED

2 TABLESPOONS PLAIN FLOUR

3/4 CUP UNOAKED CHARDONNAY

3/4 CUP FISH STOCK

1/2 CUP CREAM

1/4 CUP SALTED CAPERS,
RINSED AND DRAINED

SEA SALT AND FRESHLY GROUND
BLACK PEPPER

800G SKINLESS SNAPPER FILLETS,
CUT INTO 5CM PIECES

300G PUFF PASTRY

1 EGG, LIGHTLY BEATEN TO GLAZE

1 Heat a saucepan, add oil and onion and cook over a medium heat for 5 minutes to soften. Remove pan from the heat and stir in flour to form a smooth paste. Add wine, stirring to incorporate. Return to the heat and bring to the boil, stirring until sauce thickens. Simmer for 5 minutes to reduce wine.

2 Add fish stock and simmer for 5 minutes, stirring regularly until liquid is reduced and the sauce is smooth. Add cream and capers, and season with salt and pepper to taste. Refrigerate until cold.

3 Divide half the cold sauce between four 1 1/4 cup-capacity individual pie dishes. Cover each with 200g snapper and top with remaining sauce.

4 Roll out pastry to 3mm thick. Cut out pastry shapes slightly larger than the dishes. Brush top edge of dishes with beaten egg and place pastry over filling to form lids. Press the pastry edges to secure and pierce the pastry lids with a knife tip several times to release steam during cooking. Chill for 30 minutes.

5 Preheat oven to 200°C. Glaze pastry lids with beaten egg. Bake for 30 minutes or until pastry is puffed and golden brown. Serve immediately.

serves 4

ROCK MELON & SOFT CHEESE SALAD

Shaving the melon for this salad creates silky, featherlight slivers that are heavenly to eat and work well with the cheese, the crunchy pine nuts and salty caper berries.

½ ROCK MELON, SEEDS AND RIND REMOVED
200G CAMEMBERT OR BRIE
¼ CUP TOASTED PINE NUTS
¼ CUP CAPER BERRIES
ZEST AND JUICE OF 1 LEMON

1 Shave the melon flesh into very thin slivers – this is most easily done with a vegetable peeler. Finely slice the cheese.

2 Layer the melon with slices of soft cheese on a serving plate. Scatter with pine nuts and caper berries.

3 Drizzle the salad with lemon juice and garnish with lemon zest.

serves 4

SUBSTITUTE ...
IF YOU ARE NOT PARTIAL TO BRIE OR CAMEMBERT, TRY FETA OR GOAT'S CHEESE INSTEAD. YOU CAN ALSO OPT FOR OLIVES IN PLACE OF THE CAPER BERRIES FOR A CHANGE OR IN FACT EXCHANGE WATERMELON FOR THE ROCKMELON. I RECOMMEND EXPERIMENTING WITH THE ADDITION OF DIFFERENT HERBS TO THIS SALAD, SUCH AS MINT OR BASIL, WHICH ARE COMPLEMENTARY TO THE FLAVOUR OF MELON.

SALMON CONFIT WITH NIÇOISE VEGETABLES

Confit is a French method of preserving meat cooked in fat, with duck being the usual meat to receive this treatment. While salmon confit is not traditional, it does prove that the confit method can work well with other ingredients. The salmon flesh cooks very gently in a warm oil bath to become divinely soft and succulent. While it may sound like the finished dish will be oily, this is certainly not the case.

1 LITRE OLIVE OIL

3 CLOVES GARLIC, ROUGHLY CHOPPED

800G FRESH SALMON FILLET, SKIN AND BONES REMOVED, CUT INTO 4 PORTIONS

3 TOMATOES, SEEDS REMOVED, FINELY DICED

1 LEBANESE CUCUMBER, SEEDS REMOVED, FINELY DICED

¼ CUP PITTED BLACK OLIVES

ZEST AND JUICE OF 1 LEMON

SEA SALT AND FRESHLY GROUND BLACK PEPPER

250G ROUND FRENCH GREEN BEANS, TRIMMED

600G BABY POTATOES

1 Place olive oil and garlic in a deep pan and heat gently until tepid (blood heat when tested with the tip of a finger). Dry the salmon on paper towels and place in the oil so that it fits snugly and is covered with oil. Cook at this low temperature for only 12 minutes.

2 Remove salmon portions with a slotted spoon and drain briefly on paper towels. Combine diced tomatoes, cucumber, olives, lemon zest and juice in a bowl; season with salt and pepper and toss well.

3 Serve salmon portions on a bed of hot beans and potatoes, topped with the salsa of diced vegetables and olives.

serves 4

SERVING SUGGESTION ...
FOLLOW FRENCH TRADITION AND SERVE A MESCLUN
SALAD AS A SEPARATE COURSE TO CLEANSE THE
PALATE AFTER THE MAIN COURSE

CHERRY PISTACHIO NUT-ROAST

When you've eaten your fill of summer cherries in all their natural glory, it's worth letting a few escape into baking tins and saucepans.

1 ONION, FINELY DICED

1 CLOVE GARLIC, CRUSHED

60G BUTTER OR ¼ CUP OLIVE OIL

4 CUPS WHOLEGRAIN BREADCRUMBS

1 TEASPOON SPANISH SMOKED SWEET PAPRIKA

1 TABLESPOON CHOPPED FRESH OREGANO

½ CUP TOASTED PISTACHIO NUTS

1 CUP CHERRIES, PITTED

1 EGG, LIGHTLY BEATEN

SEA SALT AND FRESHLY GROUND BLACK PEPPER

1 In a saucepan, cook onion and garlic in butter or olive oil for 5–10 minutes until soft and translucent but not coloured. Remove from heat and mix in breadcrumbs, paprika and oregano. Preheat oven to 190°C.

2 Transfer to a bowl to cool, then mix in pistachios, cherries and beaten egg to bind mixture. Season with salt and pepper to taste.

3 Pack into a lightly oiled loaf pan and bake for 40 minutes until golden brown. Slice to serve.

serves 6

MINTED CHERRY SAUCE

This fruity savoury sauce makes a great accompaniment to roast chicken, turkey or lamb, or sliced ham.

½ CUP REDCURRANT JELLY

½ CUP ORANGE JUICE

¼ CUP PORT

1 CUP CHERRIES, PITTED

1 TABLESPOON FINELY SLICED FRESH MINT

SEA SALT AND FRESHLY GROUND BLACK PEPPER

1 Place redcurrant jelly, orange juice and port in a saucepan and bring to the boil, stirring regularly until jelly melts, then simmer for 5 minutes.

2 Add cherries and simmer for 2 minutes. Add mint and season with salt and pepper.

makes 1 cup

MY ADVICE …
CHOOSE CHERRIES THAT ARE GLOSSY,
FIRM, FAT AND HEAVY FOR THEIR SIZE;
THIS STATE INDICATES THEY HAVE BEEN
LEFT TO GROW FULLY AND RIPEN ON
THE TREE. MASS AND FLAVOUR ARE
LOST WITH EARLY PICKING SO CHERRIES
ARE BEST WHEN VOLUPTUOUSLY
FLESHY AND YIELDING TO THE TONGUE.

CHOCOLATE CHIP CHERRY CUPCAKES

Cupcakes are real nostalgia food for me, so I love that they're the height of fashion again. These little numbers, with their hidden cherry treasures, are just so deliciously cute – I know you'll find them completely irresistible.

125G BUTTER
¾ CUP SUGAR
3 SMALL EGGS
½ CUP SOUR CREAM
½ CUP CHOCOLATE CHIPS
1 CUP PLAIN FLOUR
1 TEASPOON BAKING POWDER
3 TABLESPOONS COCOA POWDER

1 Preheat oven to 180ºC (160ºC fan bake). Grease and flour 12 x 180ml-capacity muffin pans, or 36 x 50ml-capacity mini muffin pans or line with individual paper cases.

2 Cream butter and sugar until pale. Beat in eggs and sour cream.

3 Fold in chocolate chips and sifted dry ingredients. Spoon into prepared tins and poke a whole cherry into each.

4 Bake standard muffin size for 30 minutes, mini muffin size for 20 minutes.

makes 12 standard or
36 mini cakes

STRAWBERRY PRALINE TARTS

The bases of these praline tarts are chewy and fragrant and can hold any seasonal fruits. Try strawberries, raspberries, blueberries, cherries or even sliced fresh peaches. Another option is to hide a dollop of crème fraîche or custard under the fruit.

70G BUTTER, SOFTENED
70G GROUND ALMONDS
5 TABLESPOONS CASTER SUGAR
1 PUNNET LARGE STRAWBERRIES

1 Preheat oven to 180°C (160°C fan bake). Combine butter, almonds and sugar in a bowl and beat well until creamy.

2 Divide mixture between 8 shallow, old-fashioned patty pans and press with the back of a teaspoon to flatten into the pans.

3 Bake for 15–20 minutes or until golden brown – you may need to turn the tray of patty pans around half way through cooking to ensure even cooking. This almond pastry will rise during baking and then collapse to form a tart base. Remove to a wire rack to cool.

4 Place strawberries in praline tart cases. Dust with icing sugar to serve.

makes 8

MY ADVICE … TO KEEP THEM FRESH, STORE GROUND NUTS IN AN AIRTIGHT CONTAINER IN THE FRIDGE SO THAT THEY DO NOT DETERIORATE OR BECOME RANCID.

SUBSTITUTE ...
AN EQUAL QUANTITY OF
PEACHES, APRICOTS OR ANY
SUMMER BERRIES FOR THE
MANGO, IF PREFERRED.

FROZEN MANGO YOGHURT

This simple, scrumptious dessert is refreshingly low-fat.

2 MANGOES, PEELED, FLESH REMOVED FROM STONE
3 TABLESPOONS SUGAR
JUICE OF 1 LEMON
1½ CUPS LOW-FAT YOGHURT

1 Purée mango, sugar and lemon juice in a food processor.
Add yoghurt and process to combine.

2 Pour into a shallow metal dish, cover and freeze for 2 hours
until partially set. Break up and stir iced mixture. Refreeze
for 3 hours or until set.

3 Scoop into dishes to serve with fresh seasonal fruit if
desired.

serves 4

COCONUT MILK JELLIES WITH RASPBERRIES

Meltingly soft and luscious, these quivering coconut milk jellies combine the taste of the tropics with the consistency of panna cotta.

2 LEMONGRASS STALKS, OUTER LAYERS REMOVED

425ML CAN COCONUT MILK

½ CUP CREAM

3 TABLESPOONS CASTER SUGAR

5 X 2G GELATINE LEAVES

SUNFLOWER OIL TO BRUSH MOULDS

FRESH RASPBERRIES TO SERVE

1 Bruise the bulbous end of the lemongrass stalks to release their flavour. Coarsely chop the lemongrass and place in a saucepan with the coconut milk, cream and sugar. Heat this mixture, stirring until the sugar dissolves, to almost boiling but do not let it boil. Remove from the heat.

2 Meanwhile, soak the gelatine leaves in a bowl of cold water for 5 minutes until softened. Squeeze the softened gelatine leaves to remove any excess water, then add these to the hot coconut milk mixture, stirring until dissolved. Leave mixture to cool a little and for flavours to infuse, then strain to remove and discard lemongrass.

3 Very lightly brush 6 x 150ml-capacity jelly moulds or cups with a little oil. Pour the mixture into the moulds and refrigerate for at least 4 hours (or preferably overnight) to set.

4 To unmould jellies, release air-lock and invert moulds onto serving plates. It may be necessary to shake moulds to free jellies. Serve with fresh raspberries.

makes 6

MY ADVICE . . .
IF GELATINE LEAVES ARE NOT AVAILABLE, SUBSTITUTE 3 TEASPOONS GELATINE POWDER TO SET THIS AMOUNT OF LIQUID. SPRINKLE POWDERED GELATINE OVER ¼ CUP COLD WATER AND LEAVE TO SWELL. PLACE CUP IN A WATER-BATH OR MICROWAVE AND GENTLY HEAT TO MELT. POUR MELTED GELATINE INTO HOT COCONUT MILK MIXTURE AND STIR WELL TO COMBINE.

GOOD IDEA …
IF YOU WISH TO MAKE THIS DESSERT
OUT OF SEASON, OPT FOR PRESERVED
PASSIONFRUIT PULP FROM THE
SUPERMARKETS OR STOCK UP BY
FREEZING EXCESS FRESH PULP FOR
A SUPPLY OF THE REAL THING ALL
YEAR ROUND.

HONEY & PASSIONFRUIT PARFAITS

In general, the lighter honeys are milder and the darker ones are more bold-flavoured, and apart from being a natural energy source, these sweet offerings contain vitamins, minerals, antioxidants and amino acids.

¼ CUP WATER

PULP OF 6 PASSIONFRUIT

½ CUP HONEY

4 EGG YOLKS

2 TABLESPOONS SUGAR

2 TABLESPOONS BRANDY OR LIQUEUR, SUCH AS LIMONCELLO OR COINTREAU

½ CUP CREAM, LIGHTLY WHIPPED

3 EXTRA PASSIONFRUIT TO DECORATE

1 Place water, passionfruit pulp and honey in a small saucepan and bring to the boil. Boil for 2–3 minutes until thickened to form a syrup.

2 Place egg yolks and sugar in a bowl and whisk for 2 minutes. Pour in the hot syrup, little by little, whisking constantly. Continue to whisk until mixture is thick and pale and has cooled (this will take about 10 minutes). Stir in the liqueur and fold in the whipped cream.

3 Divide mixture between 6 glass parfait glasses or bowls and freeze for at least 4 hours to set. Serve each frozen parfait topped with the pulp of half a fresh passionfruit.

serves 6

LEMON BLUEBERRY SLICE

The usual way to cut slices is into squares or bars (rectangles), but I also like diamond or triangle shapes, and bite-size cubes create dainty nibbles for after-dinner. You can also transform this lemon blueberry slice into an impressive dessert by serving a portion with a dollop of vanilla ice-cream.

125G BUTTER, SOFTENED
¾ CUP CASTER SUGAR
FINELY GRATED ZEST OF 1 LEMON
2 SMALL EGGS
½ CUP SOUR CREAM
1½ CUPS SELF-RAISING FLOUR, SIFTED
1½ CUPS BLUEBERRIES
(FRESH OR FROZEN)

LEMON ICING

25G SOFTENED BUTTER
2 CUPS ICING SUGAR
JUICE OF 2 LEMONS

1 Preheat oven to 190°C (175°C fan bake). Line a 17x27cm slice tin with non-stick baking paper, allowing an overhang on all sides.

2 Beat butter, sugar and lemon zest in a bowl until pale and creamy. Beat in eggs and sour cream. Gently stir in flour to just combine. Spread into the prepared tin. Scatter blueberries over surface of cake batter.

3 Bake for 45 minutes, or until firm and golden brown. Remove to cool completely before icing.

4 To make icing, beat butter with icing sugar and lemon juice until creamy then spread over surface of slice. Cut into squares or diamonds to serve. This slice lasts 2–3 days stored in an airtight container.

makes 18

CLASSIC SPONGE CAKE WITH PASSIONFRUIT ICING

A sponge is really just a puff of perfumed air bound into the form of a cake. And that's the secret to making the perfect sponge – retaining all the air that is beaten into the initial egg and sugar mixture. My Mum passed this great recipe on to me.

3 LARGE EGGS, AT ROOM TEMPERATURE
PINCH SALT
½ CUP CASTER SUGAR
½ TEASPOON VANILLA EXTRACT
½ CUP CORNFLOUR
1 TABLESPOON FLOUR
1 TEASPOON BAKING POWDER
½ CUP CREAM, LIGHTLY WHIPPED

1 Preheat oven to 190°C (170°C fan bake). Line the bases of 2 x 20cm round cake tins with non-stick baking paper. Lightly grease the sides of the tins and dust with flour.

2 Place eggs, salt, sugar and vanilla in a large bowl and whisk with an electric beater until very thick and pale and ribbons of the mixture hold their shape.

3 Sift together the cornflour, flour and baking powder. With a large metal spoon, quickly and gently fold the sifted dry ingredients into the egg mixture. Do not over-mix at this stage or air will be lost, deflating the sponge mixture.

4 Divide mixture between the prepared tins and bake for 15–20 minutes, until the sponges test cooked. Don't insert a skewer as this will deflate the sponge. Test by pressing the surface with a fingertip – the sponge will spring back if it is cooked. The sponge will also shrink back from the sides of the tin when cooked.

5 Remove to a wire rack to cool. Once cold, sandwich together with whipped cream and drizzle surface with passionfruit icing. Slice in wedges to serve.

serves 12

BAKING TIP ...
TO PRODUCE PERFECTLY LIGHT SPONGE CAKES EVERY TIME, WORK QUICKLY ONCE THE DRY INGREDIENTS ARE ADDED. FOLD THE DRY INGREDIENTS IN GENTLY WITH A LARGE METAL SPOON, TAKING CARE NOT TO KNOCK OUT ANY AIR.

PASSIONFRUIT ICING

1½ CUPS ICING SUGAR, SIFTED
PULP OF 3 PASSIONFRUIT
1 TABLESPOON BOILING WATER

1 Place all ingredients in a bowl and stir to combine into icing that is of a pourable consistency.

autumn

THE FLAVOURS OF AUTUMN ARE EARTHY
AND ABUNDANT, NOW IS THE TIME TO TAKE
ADVANTAGE OF THE GLUT OF END-OF-SUMMER
VEGETABLES SUCH AS EGGPLANT, COURGETTES
AND PEPPERS; FORAGE FOR MUSHROOMS; AND
CRACK OPEN FRESH NUTS. COOK UP SATISFYING
FEASTS AND ENJOY THE LAST WARMTH OF THE
SUN AS OUR DAYS BEGIN TO SHORTEN.

MY ADVICE ...
THE ADDITION OF CHORIZO IS REALLY
IMPORTANT BECAUSE THIS HIGHLY
SEASONED SAUSAGE WILL EXUDE ITS
PUNGENT FLAVOUR INTO THE RICE,
INFUSING IT WITH A WARM GLOW OF
CHILLI AND AROMATIC SPICES.

CHICKEN & CHORIZO JAMBALAYA

Chicken jambalaya is a real oldie but a goodie, and makes a brilliant weeknight meal as it can be ready to eat in under 30 minutes.

OLIVE OIL

600G SKINLESS CHICKEN BREASTS, THINLY SLICED

1 RED ONION, DICED

2 CLOVES GARLIC, CHOPPED

1 RED PEPPER, SEEDS REMOVED, DICED

1 GREEN PEPPER, SEEDS REMOVED, DICED

3 CHORIZO SAUSAGES, SLICED

1 1/2 CUPS LONG GRAIN RICE

2 TEASPOONS SWEET SPANISH SMOKED PAPRIKA

1 1/2 CUPS TOMATO PURÉE

2 CUPS CHICKEN STOCK

1/4 CUP CHOPPED PARSLEY

SEA SALT AND FRESHLY GROUND BLACK PEPPER

1 Heat a large pan, add a little oil and brown sliced chicken; remove to one side.

2 In the same pan cook onion, garlic and diced pepper for 5 minutes, stirring often. Add chorizo, rice and paprika and stir-fry for 1–2 minutes. Add tomato purée and stock. Bring to the boil, then cover and simmer gently for 20 minutes.

3 Fluff up rice and stir in chicken and parsley; season with salt and pepper to taste. Cover and stand for 5 minutes for chicken to warm through. Serve immediately.

serves 6

SUBSTITUTE ...
DIFFERENT INGREDIENTS FOR THE
PUMPKIN FILLING IF DESIRED. TRY ROAST
SWEET POTATO WITH CARAMELISED
ONIONS; PITTED OLIVES AND CRUMBLED
BLUE CHEESE; OR SHAVED PARMESAN.

PUMPKIN, PROSCIUTTO & PEPPER PIES

It is often a good idea to buy pumpkin that has been cut into manageable portions – this way you can see inside and judge how flavourful the pumpkin will be. Look for a strong depth of colour and firm flesh that is not watery and you will be rewarded with great flavour.

800G PEELED BUTTERNUT PUMPKIN

¼ CUP OLIVE OIL

SEA SALT AND FRESHLY GROUND
BLACK PEPPER

400G SAVOURY SHORTCRUST PASTRY

100G PROSCIUTTO, ROUGHLY CHOPPED

100G FETA, ROUGHLY CUBED

2 TABLESPOONS CHOPPED FRESH
OREGANO

6 MINIATURE RED PEPPERS
(OR SUBSTITUTE 2 RED PEPPERS),
SEEDS REMOVED, CUBED

6 BASIL LEAVES TO GARNISH

1 Preheat oven to 200°C. Cut pumpkin into 2cm cubes and place in an oven pan. Toss with olive oil and season well with salt and pepper. Roast for 30 minutes until golden brown, tossing once during cooking. Remove to cool.

2 At the same time, roll out pastry to 3mm thick on a lightly floured surface. Cut pastry into 6 x 18cm squares and fit one into each of the 6 holes of a Texas muffin pan. Prick the bases and refrigerate for 30 minutes.

3 Line the pastry cases with non-stick baking paper and baking beans to bake blind for 15 minutes at 200°C. Remove the baking beans and paper, turn the oven down to 180°C and bake the pastry cases for a further 5 minutes.

4 Combine the cubes of roast pumpkin with the prosciutto, feta and oregano. Rub the peppers with a little oil and place one on top of each pie and bake for 15 minutes. Remove from the oven and garnish each finished pie with a basil leaf.

makes 6

GINGER CHICKEN & CRISPY NOODLE STIR-FRY

Stir-fries are the modern person's mid-week meal solution. They are vibrant, healthy and can be put together in next to no time. Plus, the possible flavour combinations are seemingly endless. Here, chicken is flavoured with fresh ginger, and crispy noodles create textural contrast.

1 TABLESPOON SESAME OIL

1 TABLESPOON SUNFLOWER OIL

3 LARGE SKINLESS CHICKEN BREASTS, SLICED

3 TABLESPOONS GRATED FRESH GINGER

1 BUNCH SPRING ONIONS, CUT INTO 4CM LENGTHS

3 RED PEPPERS, SEEDS REMOVED, CUT INTO PIECES

150G GREEN BEANS, TRIMMED

400G CAN BABY SWEETCORN, DRAINED

3–4 TABLESPOONS LIGHT SOY SAUCE

140G PACKET CRISPY NOODLES

3 TABLESPOONS TOASTED WHITE OR BLACK SESAME SEEDS

1 Heat a wok or large frying pan, add oils and chicken and stir-fry for a few minutes, tossing well over a high heat to brown. Remove to one side.

2 Add ginger and vegetables, toss and stir-fry for 5 minutes to brown. Return chicken to the pan, add soy sauce and a little water if necessary to finish cooking vegetables.

3 Lastly, add crispy noodles and stir-fry briefly to heat through. Sprinkle with sesame seeds and serve immediately.

serves 4

MY ADVICE …
BEFORE STARTING TO STIR-FRY, DO ALL THE SLICING, CHOPPING AND BLANCHING NECESSARY TO PREPARE INGREDIENTS FOR THIS FAST-COOKING TECHNIQUE. HEAT THE WOK BEFORE ADDING ANY OIL SO THAT THE OIL DOES NOT BURN, THEN ADD THE FOOD IMMEDIATELY. IT IS BEST TO COOK FOOD IN BATCHES SO THAT IT BROWNS – THIS AVOIDS LOWERING THE WOK'S TEMPERATURE, WHICH CAN CAUSE THE FOOD TO STEW. DEVELOP A DEFT TOUCH FOR STIR-FRYING BY LIFTING, TOSSING AND STIRRING THE FOOD WITH A SHOVEL-LIKE UTENSIL (CALLED A WOK CHAN) SO THAT IT COOKS QUICKLY WITHOUT STICKING OR BURNING. WOK-COOKED FOOD IS BEST SERVED AND EATEN IMMEDIATELY.

CHICKPEA, EGGPLANT & GOAT'S CHEESE SALAD

While this salad forms a perfect vegetarian meal, it can also work well as a side dish to meat, for example, roast chicken. Like companionable friendship, this sort of unhurried weekend lunch food is good for the soul.

500G (1 LARGE) EGGPLANT

¼ CUP OLIVE OIL

2 X 400G CANS CHICKPEAS, RINSED AND DRAINED

200G GOAT'S CHEESE, SLICED

½ CUP TORN BASIL LEAVES

1 Preheat oven to 200°C. Slice eggplant into 5mm rounds and brush lightly with olive oil on both sides. Place on an oven tray and bake for 15 minutes until golden brown, turning once during cooking. Set aside to cool.

2 Combine cold eggplant, chickpeas, and goat's cheese in a salad bowl. Mix dressing ingredients together and pour over salad. Season with salt and pepper to taste and toss well to serve. Garnish with basil leaves.

serves 4

TOMATO & BALSAMIC DRESSING

2 LARGE TOMATOES, SEEDS REMOVED, FINELY DICED

¼ CUP EXTRA VIRGIN OLIVE OIL

3–4 TABLESPOONS QUALITY BALSAMIC VINEGAR

SEA SALT AND FRESHLY GROUND BLACK PEPPER

SUBSTITUTE …
IF YOU WISH TO REDUCE THE AMOUNT OF OIL IN ANY SALAD DRESSING, COUNTER-BALANCE THIS BY USING PLENTY OF HERBS, CITRUS RIND OR SPICES TO PROVIDE FLAVOUR INSTEAD OF FAT.

COURGETTE & AGED CHEDDAR SLICE

Slices are so versatile – they can serve as picnic food; school or work lunch-box treats; something to share at coffee morning; or as a late-night snack. Try this courgette and aged Cheddar slice for brunch with chutney on the side.

2 TABLESPOONS OLIVE OIL

1 MEDIUM ONION, FINELY SLICED

500G (4 MEDIUM) COURGETTES, GRATED

1 TABLESPOON CHOPPED FRESH OREGANO

¾ CUP GRATED AGED CHEDDAR

1 CUP SELF-RAISING FLOUR

4 EGGS

1 CUP MILK

SEA SALT AND FRESHLY GROUND
BLACK PEPPER

3 MEDIUM TOMATOES, THINLY SLICED

1 Preheat oven to 200°C. Line a 17x27cm slice tin with non-stick baking paper, allowing an overhang on all sides.

2 Heat oil in a frying pan and cook the onion for 5 minutes until softened but not coloured. Remove to cool. Squeeze any excess liquid from the grated courgettes and add to the cooled onion with the oregano, cheese and flour.

3 In another bowl, lightly beat the eggs with the milk and season with salt and pepper. Stir wet ingredients into dry ingredients and mix to just combine. Pour into prepared tin. Arrange tomato slices on top.

4 Bake for 40 minutes or until firm in the centre. Cool in the tin for 10 minutes to firm before turning out to slice. Lasts for up to 3 days if stored in the fridge.

serves 8–10

CHORIZO, PORK & BASIL ROLLO

I love the tradition of Spanish tapas, which incorporates an entire range of bar snacks to be enjoyed with a glass of chilled sherry (another Andalusian specialty). While this is an old tradition, today tapas can be just about any food served in small portions, such as this Spanish-inspired recipe.

3 LARGE PORK SCHNITZELS

½ CUP LARGE BASIL LEAVES, TIGHTLY PACKED

3–6 CHORIZO (DEPENDING ON SIZE) – ENOUGH TO FIT THE PORK

SEA SALT AND FRESHLY GROUND BLACK PEPPER

1 Lay pork schnitzels on a board (pound to flatten if necessary). Arrange basil leaves to cover pork. Place a chorizo at one lengthways end and roll up so that pork totally covers chorizo. Tie rolls with string to secure and season with salt and pepper.

2 Preheat oven to 200°C. Heat a little oil in a frying pan, fry rolls for 5 minutes over a medium heat until browned all over.

3 Remove to an oven pan and roast for 10 minutes. Remove to cool a little before slicing each roll into 5–6 equal portions. Skewer portions to serve.

serves 4–6 as a snack

HOW TO MAKE …
ROASTED ALMONDS LIKE THE ONES THAT ARE
COMPLEMENTARY IN MANY SPANISH BARS. PLACE
A CUP OF BLANCHED ALMONDS IN AN OVEN PAN
AND DRY ROAST IN AN OVEN PREHEATED TO 160°C
FOR 15–20 MINUTES, OR UNTIL GOLDEN BROWN.
REMOVE AND DRIZZLE WITH A LITTLE OLIVE OIL,
DUST WITH SEA SALT AND TOSS WELL TO COAT.

TOMATO & ANCHOVY RISOTTO

I only buy plain canned tomatoes as opposed to the raft of pre-flavoured ones because I prefer to add my own fresh herbs, spices and other seasonings. This way I produce the flavours I want and I know exactly what has gone into the dish. I am keen on the cans of conveniently diced tomatoes though, as I like to avoid all that messy chopping-up.

3 CUPS CHICKEN STOCK
400G CAN TOMATOES, CHOPPED
2 TABLESPOONS OLIVE OIL
2 CLOVES GARLIC, CRUSHED
1 ONION, FINELY DICED
1 ½ CUPS RISOTTO RICE (I USE CARNAROLI OR VIALONE NANO)
8 ANCHOVIES, CHOPPED
½ CUP FRESHLY GRATED PARMESAN
SEA SALT AND FRESHLY GROUND BLACK PEPPER
EXTRA PARMESAN TO SERVE

1 Heat stock and tomatoes and their juice together in a saucepan.

2 Heat a large heavy-based pan, add oil, garlic and onion and cook gently for 5 minutes. Add rice and stir for 2 minutes to toast but not brown. Add one ladleful of hot stock and stir well. When the rice has absorbed the liquid, add another ladleful of stock.

3 Continue to stir and keep adding hot liquid until it is all absorbed. After 15–20 minutes the rice should be al dente and creamy.

4 Stir in anchovies and Parmesan, and season with salt and pepper to taste. Cover pan and leave to steam for 5 minutes. Serve with extra Parmesan if desired.

serves 4

SHORTCUT …
TOMATOES ARE CANNED AT THEIR PEAK WHEN THEY ARE FULL OF FLAVOUR – PLUS, IF THEY HAPPEN TO BE ITALIAN TOMATOES, SUN-RIPENED ON THE VINE AND PRESERVED IN ITALY, I FIGURE THERE'S A HEALTHY AMOUNT OF ITALIAN SUNSHINE PACKED INTO THE CAN AS WELL.

CHICKEN CACCIATORE

Chicken cacciatore or hunter's-style chicken is a classic American-Italian dish. While recipes for this dish will vary from cook to cook, the common denominators are always tomatoes and chicken stewed until it's so tender it nearly falls from the bone.

2 TABLESPOONS OLIVE OIL

6 CHICKEN LEGS, DRUMSTICK AND THIGH SEPARATED

1 ONION, SLICED

1 RED PEPPER, SEEDS REMOVED, CHOPPED

3 CLOVES GARLIC, CHOPPED

½ CUP RED WINE

½ CUP CHICKEN STOCK

2 TABLESPOONS TOMATO PASTE

2 X 400G CANS TOMATOES, CRUSHED

½ CUP PITTED BLACK OLIVES

2 TABLESPOONS CHOPPED FRESH OREGANO

SEA SALT AND FRESHLY GROUND BLACK PEPPER

1 Heat a large heavy-based pan, add oil and brown chicken in 2–3 batches for 2–3 minutes on each side. Remove to one side. Add onion, pepper and garlic and cook for 5 minutes to soften but not colour.

2 Stir in wine, stock, tomato paste and canned tomatoes and bring to the boil. Add chicken, cover and simmer gently for 1 hour or until very tender.

3 Add olives and oregano and simmer uncovered for 10 minutes to thicken sauce. Adjust seasoning with salt and pepper to taste. Serve with plain fettuccine and steamed greens.

serves 6

GOOD IDEA ...
TRY POURING A CAN OF CRUSHED TOMATOES OVER A WHOLE CHICKEN OR PIECE OF MEAT BEFORE ROASTING IN THE USUAL WAY. ADD A LITTLE OLIVE OIL AND SOME STOCK OR WINE AND BASTE THE MEAT DURING COOKING TO PRODUCE A SUCCULENT ROAST AND WONDERFUL CARAMELISED TOMATO SAUCE.

GREEN LENTIL SALAD WITH LEMON CHILLI DRESSING

I particularly enjoy creating flavoursome vegetable dishes and some of my most favourite meals are structured around pulses, grains and lentils.

½ CUP GREEN LENTILS

2 RED PEPPERS, SEEDS REMOVED, FINELY SLICED

250G GREEN BEANS, TRIMMED AND BLANCHED

2 CUPS BABY SPINACH OR ROCKET LEAVES

¼ CUP CAPERS

1 Place lentils in a saucepan with plenty of cold water and bring to the boil. Turn down the heat and simmer for 20 minutes or until lentils are just tender. Drain well and set aside to cool.

2 Place cooled lentils and remaining salad ingredients in a bowl. Blend dressing ingredients together and season with salt and pepper to taste. Pour dressing over salad and toss well.

serves 4

LEMON CHILLI DRESSING

¼ CUP EXTRA VIRGIN OLIVE OIL

1 RED CHILLI, SEEDS REMOVED, FINELY CHOPPED

JUICE OF 2 LEMONS

SEA SALT AND FRESHLY GROUND BLACK PEPPER

MY ADVICE...
DRIED GREEN LENTILS DO NOT REQUIRE SOAKING BEFORE COOKING. WHEN COOKING LENTILS OR PULSES, DON'T ADD SALT TO THE COOKING WATER AS THIS CAN MAKE THEM TOUGH – ALWAYS SEASON THE COMPLETED DISH INSTEAD.

MY ADVICE ...
DRINK JASMINE OR GREEN TEA OR
LAGER WITH ASIAN FLAVOURS. IF YOU
PREFER TO DRINK WINE, THEN THESE
FRAGRANT ASIAN DISHES DEMAND
AROMATIC WINES SUCH AS DRY RIESLING,
GEWÜRZTRAMINER OR PINOT GRIS.

SEAFOOD LAKSA

This classic Malaysian rice noodle soup has become a favourite meal-in-a-bowl, internationally.

3 CLOVES GARLIC, CHOPPED

3CM PIECE FRESH GINGER, PEELED
AND CHOPPED

1 SMALL RED CHILLI, SEEDS REMOVED,
CHOPPED

1 TABLESPOON PALM SUGAR OR
BROWN SUGAR

1 TEASPOON GROUND TURMERIC

¼ CUP ROASTED CASHEW NUTS

JUICE OF 2 LIMES

3 TABLESPOONS PEANUT OR
SUNFLOWER OIL

2 CUPS QUALITY FISH, VEGETABLE
OR CHICKEN STOCK

400ML CAN COCONUT MILK

12 PEELED GREEN PRAWNS

400G WHITE FISH, CUBED

100G RICE VERMICELLI NOODLES,
SOAKED FOR 10 MINUTES IN HOT WATER

2–4 TABLESPOONS THAI FISH SAUCE
TO TASTE

2 SPRING ONIONS, FINELY SLICED

EXTRA FINELY SLICED RED CHILLI TO SERVE

1 Grind first 7 ingredients in a mortar and pestle or in a food processor to form a spice paste. Heat a large heavy-based saucepan, add oil and spice paste and cook over a medium heat for 1–2 minutes so that flavours are released.

2 Add stock and bring to the boil, then simmer for 10 minutes. Add coconut milk and simmer for a further 5 minutes. Add seafood and simmer for 5 minutes to cook.

3 Drain noodles and add, then simmer for 2 minutes to heat through. Season with fish sauce to taste. Ladle into bowls and garnish with spring onions and extra chilli if desired.

serves 4

SHAOXING RICE WINE ...
IS A CHINESE WINE MADE FROM RICE,
MILLET AND YEAST. IT IS READILY
AVAILABLE IN ASIAN GROCERY STORES
AND SOME SUPERMARKETS BUT
YOU CAN SUBSTITUTE DRY SHERRY,
IF NECESSARY.

SWEET & SOUR FISH

Sweet and sour flavours are very popular and they complement the lightness of freshly fried fish beautifully.

600G FIRM WHITE-FLESHED FISH FILLETS, SUCH AS SNAPPER OR COD

1/2 TEASPOON SEA SALT

2 TABLESPOONS SHAOXING RICE WINE

1 EGG, BEATEN

1/3 CUP RICE FLOUR OR PLAIN FLOUR

PEANUT OR SUNFLOWER OIL FOR DEEP-FRYING

CORIANDER LEAVES TO GARNISH

SWEET & SOUR SAUCE

1 TABLESPOON FINELY GRATED FRESH GINGER

1/2 CUP CHICKEN STOCK

3 TABLESPOONS LIGHT SOY SAUCE

2 TABLESPOONS SUGAR

3 TABLESPOONS RICE VINEGAR

1 RED CHILLI, SEEDS REMOVED, FINELY CHOPPED

1 TABLESPOON CORNFLOUR DISSOLVED IN 2 TABLESPOONS COLD WATER

1 TEASPOON SESAME OIL

1 Dry the fish by patting with paper towels. Cut into 3cm cubes and combine with the salt and rice wine to marinate in a bowl for 20 minutes.

2 Blend the egg and flour with enough water to form a smooth batter with the consistency of thick cream. Toss the cubed fish in the batter.

3 Heat a wok or pan one-third full of oil until a piece of bread when added bubbles and quickly fries to golden brown. Fry battered fish in batches in the hot oil, making sure the pieces don't stick together – cook for about 3 minutes or until golden brown. Remove to drain on paper towels and keep warm.

4 Place the sauce ingredients in another saucepan. Bring to the boil, then simmer until thickened. Pour this sauce over the fish and garnish with coriander.

serves 4

PEANUT SATAY SAUCE

I'm sure you'll enjoy the easy and satisfying process of making your own classic satay sauce – the perfect tasty complement to skewered meats or vegetable dishes such as gado-gado.

2 TABLESPOONS PEANUT OIL
1/2 SMALL ONION, FINELY DICED
2 CLOVES GARLIC, CHOPPED
1 RED CHILLI, SEEDS REMOVED, CHOPPED
1 TABLESPOON BROWN SUGAR
1 TABLESPOON DARK SOY SAUCE
JUICE OF 1 LEMON
1 CUP ROASTED PEANUTS
1 CUP COLD WATER

1 Heat oil in a saucepan, add onion and garlic and cook over a medium heat for 5 minutes until softened, but not coloured. Add chilli, brown sugar, soy sauce and lemon juice and cook for 1 minute.

2 Purée this mixture with the roasted peanuts and cold water in a blender to form a thick paste. Return paste to the saucepan and simmer for 5 minutes to reduce and thicken.

3 Satay sauce will last for up to 4 days in the fridge. Gently reheat before serving.

makes 2 cups

MY ADVICE ...
BUY NUTS IN SMALL QUANTITIES, AS AND WHEN YOU NEED THEM. NUTS HAVE A HIGH NATURAL OIL CONTENT AND THIS CAN TURN RANCID OVER TIME OR WITH EXPOSURE TO HEAT.

MOORISH CHICKEN BAKED IN ALMOND SAUCE

My Moorish chicken dish demonstrates the Spanish innovation of using ground almonds to thicken and add texture to sauces.

4 WHOLE CHICKEN LEGS

SEA SALT AND FRESHLY GROUND BLACK PEPPER

3 TABLESPOONS OLIVE OIL

4 SMALL RED ONIONS, CUT INTO WEDGES

1 RED PEPPER, SEEDS REMOVED, CUT INTO STRIPS

1/2 CUP DRY SHERRY

1/4 TEASPOON SAFFRON THREADS INFUSED IN
1/4 CUP BOILING WATER

400G CAN CHOPPED TOMATOES

1 CUP BLANCHED ALMONDS, LIGHTLY TOASTED
AND ROUGHLY GROUND

1 TABLESPOON FRESH THYME LEAVES

1 Preheat oven to 180°C. Joint the chicken legs by separating the drumsticks from the thighs. Season with salt and pepper and place in an oven pan.

2 Heat a large frying pan, add oil, onions and pepper and cook for 5 minutes, tossing frequently over a medium heat. Add sherry and simmer to reduce by half. Add saffron and liquid, and tomatoes. Stir in almonds to thicken sauce and bring to the boil.

3 Pour sauce over chicken and bake for 50–60 minutes or until chicken tests cooked (the juices will run clear when a knife is inserted to the bone into the thickest part of the meat). Adjust seasoning with salt and pepper before serving scattered with fresh thyme.

serves 4

MY ADVICE …
WHEN FEEDING NEW ACQUAINTANCES, I STEER AWAY FROM COOKING WITH NUTS BECAUSE SOME PEOPLE CAN SUFFER SEVERE ALLERGIC REACTIONS TO THEM. HOWEVER, FOR THOSE WHO PARTAKE, THE CULINARY POSSIBILITIES ARE VAST AS NUTS ARE SO WONDERFULLY VERSATILE.

DRY POTATO CURRY

Do try fresh curry leaves, as they add a unique spicy scent and taste to curry or rice dishes.

2 TABLESPOONS VEGETABLE OIL

1 TEASPOON EACH CUMIN, FENNEL
AND MUSTARD SEEDS

1 TEASPOON EACH GROUND CORIANDER
AND TURMERIC POWDER

1/2 TEASPOON CHILLI POWDER

1/3 CUP FRESH CURRY LEAVES (IF AVAILABLE)

1 RED PEPPER, SEEDS REMOVED, SLICED

400G BABY POTATOES, BOILED UNTIL TENDER

2 CUPS FROZEN PEAS, DEFROSTED

1/2 CUP VEGETABLE STOCK OR WATER

SEA SALT AND FRESHLY GROUND
BLACK PEPPER

1 Blend oil with all seeds and spices to form a yellow curry paste.

2 Heat a large pan, add curry paste and curry leaves and cook for 1 minute until seeds begin to pop and the spices are fragrant.

3 Add sliced pepper, cooked potatoes, peas and stock or water. Stir-fry for 5–7 minutes, tossing constantly until vegetables heat through. Season with salt and pepper to taste.

serves 4

SERVING SUGGESTION ...
I LIKE TO SERVE PAPPADOMS WITH
CURRIES AND FRAGRANT RICE SUCH AS
BASMATI OR JASMINE ON THE SIDE.
BOWLS OF CHOPPED FRESH CORIANDER
OR BASIL, DICED TOMATO AND CHILLI,
RAITA (PLAIN YOGHURT MIXED WITH
CUCUMBER AND CHOPPED MINT), NUTS,
SEEDS AND FRUIT CHUTNEY SUCH AS
MANGO OR APRICOT ARE ALL GREAT
ACCOMPANIMENTS TO CURRY.

RED CHICKEN CURRY

I particularly enjoy cooking curry when friends pop around for dinner because I can prepare it in advance – and it allows me to set the table with bowls of interesting condiments. This way, curry forms the centre of a wonderfully interactive meal, where everyone can share dishes and adorn their plates with tasty extras.

1 LARGE ONION, DICED

4CM PIECE FRESH GINGER, PEELED AND ROUGHLY CHOPPED

2 CLOVES GARLIC, CHOPPED

1–2 SMALL RED CHILLIES, SEEDS REMOVED

½ CUP TOMATO PURÉE

1 TEASPOON EACH GROUND CUMIN, PAPRIKA AND GARAM MASALA

3–4 TABLESPOONS SUNFLOWER OR CANOLA OIL

4 SKINLESS CHICKEN BREASTS, THINLY SLICED

1½ CUPS CHICKEN STOCK

SEA SALT AND FRESHLY GROUND BLACK PEPPER

¼ CUP CHOPPED FRESH CORIANDER

1 Place onion, ginger, garlic, chillies, tomato pureé and all spices in a food processor and blend to form a red curry paste.

2 Heat oil in a large saucepan and cook sliced chicken, tossing to brown all over. This may need to be completed in 2–3 batches. Remove chicken to one side. Add prepared red curry paste to the pan and cook for 1–2 minutes.

3 Return chicken to the pan with the stock. Bring to the boil, then gently simmer, uncovered, for 15 minutes until liquid is reduced to a rich sauce and chicken is tender.

4 Season with salt and pepper to taste. Serve scattered with fresh coriander and with fragrant basmati rice on the side.

serves 4

CARAMEL WALNUT TART

Through experimentation you will find that different nuts are easily interchangeable in recipes. For instance, macadamias, hazelnuts, pecans, Brazil nuts and even pine nuts can be used instead of the walnuts in this caramel tart. Whichever one you choose, people will certainly go nutty over this sweet treat.

300G SWEET SHORT PASTRY
1 1/4 CUPS WALNUT PIECES
100G BUTTER, SOFTENED
1/2 CUP CASTER SUGAR
3 SMALL EGGS
3/4 CUP GOLDEN SYRUP
100ML CREAM
2 TABLESPOONS FLOUR

1 Roll out pastry to 3mm thick and use to line the base and sides of a 20cm fluted tart tin. Prick the base with a fork and chill for 30 minutes.

2 Preheat oven to 210°C (190°C fan bake). Line pastry with non-stick baking paper or foil and fill with dried beans. Bake blind for 15 minutes, then remove beans and paper or foil and return pastry case to the oven for a further 5 minutes to dry out. Decrease oven temperature to 180°C (160°C fan bake).

3 Sprinkle walnuts over pastry base. Place butter and sugar in a bowl and beat with an electric mixer until pale and creamy. Beat in eggs one at a time to combine. Gently beat in golden syrup, cream and flour.

4 Pour this mixture over the nuts. Bake for 45 minutes or until caramel is just set. Cool before removing from tart tin. Slice to serve with whipped cream if desired.

serves 10

GOOD IDEA …
FRESH NUTS NOT ONLY TASTE FANTASTIC BUT ARE ALSO FULL OF HEALTH BENEFITS. THE INCLUSION OF CASHEWS IN YOUR DIET CAN HELP INCREASE VITALITY; ALMONDS CAN LIFT LOW MOODS AND COUNTER SLEEPLESSNESS; AND WALNUTS CAN IMPROVE METABOLISM.

LITTLE GINGERBREAD CAKES

Powdered ginger is traditional in gingerbread but crystallised ginger is also great to use in baking. You can either hide some in the gingerbread batter or use some to decorate these little cakes when completed, as I have done.

½ CUP GOLDEN SYRUP

¼ CUP WATER

50G BUTTER

¼ CUP TIGHTLY PACKED BROWN SUGAR

1 CUP PLAIN FLOUR

2 TEASPOONS CINNAMON

2 TEASPOONS GROUND GINGER

½ TEASPOON BAKING SODA

¼ CUP CRYSTALLISED GINGER, SLICED

1 Preheat oven to 175°C. Grease a 6-hole standard muffin pan.

2 Combine golden syrup, water, butter and brown sugar in a saucepan. Heat until butter melts and sugar has dissolved. Remove from the heat to cool completely.

3 Sift dry ingredients together in a mixing bowl. Stir golden syrup mixture into dry ingredients just enough to form a smooth batter. Do not overmix or the resulting cakes will be tough.

4 Spoon into prepared pans. Bake for 20 minutes or until cakes spring back when pressed with a fingertip. Decorate with sliced crystallised ginger.

makes 6

CHOCOLATE DATE CRUMBLE SLICE

A slice is a distinct baked goodie made in a slab pan – it's a crossbreed – being more dense than a biscuit but less substantial than cake. I find that slices are easy and pleasing treats that everyone can create with great success – their appeal lies as much in the making as it does in the eating.

400G PACKET PITTED DATES
FINELY GRATED ZEST OF 1 LEMON
1 1/2 CUPS WATER
1/2 CUP CHOCOLATE CHIPS
1 CUP FLOUR
1 CUP TIGHTLY PACKED BROWN SUGAR
185G BUTTER, CUBED
1/2 CUP FINE DESICCATED COCONUT
1/2 TEASPOON BAKING SODA
1 1/2 CUPS ROLLED OATS
2 TABLESPOONS COCOA POWDER

1 Place dates, lemon zest and water in a saucepan and bring to the boil, then simmer for 15 minutes, stirring regularly, until liquid has reduced and dates are soft. Remove to cool. Stir chocolate chips into cold date mixture.

2 Preheat oven to 190°C. Line a 17x27cm slice tin with non-stick baking paper allowing an overhang on all sides.

3 Place flour and brown sugar in the bowl of a food processor. Add the butter and process until the mixture resembles breadcrumbs. Transfer to a large bowl and stir in the coconut, baking soda and rolled oats. Reserve half the mixture. Mix the cocoa powder with the remaining mixture and press this firmly into the base of the prepared tin.

4 Spread evenly with the date filling and sprinkle with reserved mixture to form a crumble. Bake for 45 minutes or until golden brown. Cool completely before slicing. Lasts for up to 5 days if stored in an airtight container.

makes 18

TARTE TATIN

The Tatin sisters from their Hotel Tatin in Lamotte-Beuvron, France, created this caramel-sweet apple pie during the 19th century. Whether myth or legend, some say that the sisters invented this upside-down apple tart by accident, when they dropped an apple pie on the floor and saved it by serving it with the pastry on the base and the apples on top. I've had the pleasure of eating tarte Tatin at the Hotel Tatin and visiting the kitchen where the famous sisters worked.

PASTRY

1¼ CUPS PLAIN FLOUR
100G COLD BUTTER, CUBED
2 TEASPOONS FINELY GRATED LEMON ZEST
2 TABLESPOONS SUGAR
PINCH SALT
2 TABLESPOONS ICE-COLD WATER

1 Place flour in a bowl and rub in butter with your fingertips until crumbly (or this can be done in a food processor). Stir in lemon zest, sugar, salt, and then the water to combine into a firm dough.

2 Turn dough out onto a board and knead lightly. Wrap in plastic wrap and chill for 30 minutes. Roll out pastry on a lightly floured board to form a circle 25cm in diameter and 5mm thick. Prick pastry all over with a fork and remove to one side until required.

CARAMELISED APPLES

5–6 COOKING APPLES, PEELED, QUARTERED AND CORED
50G BUTTER
1 TABLESPOON WATER
¾ CUP SUGAR

1 Preheat oven to 200°C. Smear 50g butter over the base of a 24cm frying pan with an ovenproof handle. Add measured water and sugar, then arrange apples, rounded side down, in the pan. Place the pan over a medium-hot element for 10–15 minutes, shaking regularly until the butter and sugar have caramelised and turned golden brown.

2 Lay the pastry circle over the apples (the loose fit is to allow for shrinkage during cooking) and bake for 30 minutes or until the pastry is golden brown.

3 Remove pan from the oven, allow tart to firm in the pan for 2–3 minutes before inverting onto a serving plate so that the fruit is on the surface. Serve warm.

MY ADVICE ...
A GOOD TARTE TATIN MUST HAVE DEEPLY CARAMELISED APPLES AND SHOULD BE SERVED DELICIOUSLY WARM – CREAM ON THE SIDE IS AN OPTION, THOUGH IT IS HARDLY NECESSARY BECAUSE THE APPLES BECOME MELTINGLY TENDER.

serves 6–8

LADY GREY HAZELNUT FRIANDS

This recipe for Lady Grey hazelnut friands comes from the Twinings collection. The mixture includes a liberal dose of Twinings Lady Grey Tea – a blend that contains distinctive citrus flavours that complement hazelnuts beautifully.

1 CUP HAZELNUT MEAL (GROUND HAZELNUTS)

¾ CUP SELF-RAISING FLOUR, SIFTED

1¾ CUPS ICING SUGAR, SIFTED

1 TEASPOON FINELY GRATED ORANGE RIND

1½ TABLESPOONS TWININGS LADY GREY TEA LEAVES

125G BUTTER

5 EGG WHITES, LIGHTLY BEATEN

ICING SUGAR TO DUST

1 Preheat oven to 180°C (160°C fan bake). Combine the hazelnut meal, flour, icing sugar, orange rind and Twinings Lady Grey Tea in a bowl.

2 Heat the butter in a small saucepan over a medium heat until melted and light golden in colour. Cool slightly, then pour into the flour mixture, along with the egg whites, and stir until fully combined.

3 Pour the mixture into 10 lightly greased friand pans or 180ml-capacity muffin pans and bake for 15–20 minutes or until golden and springy. Cool in tins for 10 minutes, then transfer to a wire cooling rack. Dust with icing sugar to serve.

makes 10

GOOD IDEA …
I DON'T KNOW WHEN THE CONCEPT OF COOKING
WITH TEA BEGAN BUT I CAN HIGHLY RECOMMEND
TEA AS AN INGREDIENT. TEA ADDS SUBTLETY,
PERFUME AND TEXTURE TO BAKED GOODS – AND
A FLAVOUR THAT LINKS THE FOOD TO THE DRINK.

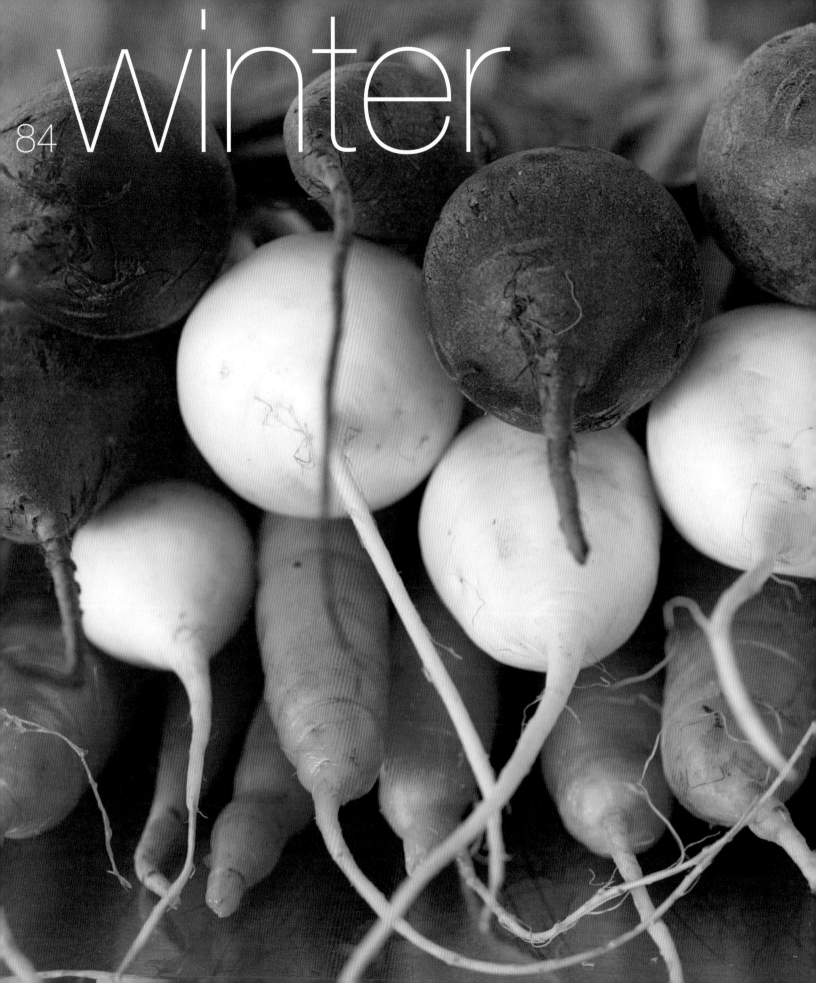

winter

COLD WINTER NIGHTS ARE THE PERFECT TIME TO INVITE FRIENDS OVER TO ENJOY GREAT FOOD AND COMPANY. THE KITCHEN IS A COSY PLACE TO GATHER WHILE GENEROUS, WARMING FOOD IS PREPARED. TAKE ADVANTAGE OF ROBUST WINTER PRODUCE AND CREATE RICH, SOUL-SATISFYING MEALS TO BOLSTER SPIRITS OVER THE YEAR'S COOLER MONTHS.

PAPRIKA PORK WITH POTATOES & SPINACH

Smoked Spanish paprika is made from a special variety of pimiento that is smoked slowly over oak. It has an intense smoky flavour and is quite different to the more familiar Hungarian variety. I use the La Chinata brand.

2 TABLESPOONS OLIVE OIL

600G PORK SHOULDER STEAKS, CUT INTO 4CM PIECES

6 SLICES RINDLESS BACON, ROUGHLY CHOPPED

2 CLOVES GARLIC, CHOPPED

1 TABLESPOON SWEET SMOKED SPANISH PAPRIKA

½ CUP RED WINE OR WATER

1½ CUPS REDUCED BEEF STOCK

6 MEDIUM WAXY POTATOES, QUARTERED LENGTHWAYS

140G PACKET BABY SPINACH LEAVES

SEA SALT AND FRESHLY GROUND BLACK PEPPER

1 In a large saucepan, add oil and brown pork pieces in batches for 1 minute on each side. Remove to one side and add bacon to the pan, tossing to brown for 2–3 minutes. Add garlic and paprika and cook for 1 minute.

2 Add wine or water and simmer for 2–3 minutes, stirring to loosen sediment from the bottom of the pan, then add the stock.

3 Return pork to the pan with the potatoes, cover and simmer very gently for 35–40 minutes or until potatoes and pork are tender.

4 Adjust seasoning with salt and pepper to taste. Just before serving, stir in spinach to wilt.

serves 4

MY ADVICE ...
FOR RECIPES THAT REQUIRE SIMMERING FOR SOME TIME, IT'S BEST TO ADD SEASONING TOWARDS THE END OF COOKING. AS THE FOOD COOKS, LIQUIDS REDUCE AND FLAVOURS ARE CONCENTRATED, SO FOR EXAMPLE, SALTINESS IS ESPECIALLY HEIGHTENED. REMEMBER YOU CAN ALWAYS ADD MORE SEASONING TO TASTE BUT IT'S DIFFICULT TO REMOVE ANY EXCESS.

MY ADVICE …
HONEY CAN BE MEASURED EASILY BY
USING THE SAME CUP USED FOR
MEASURING THE OIL IN A RECIPE OR BY
COATING A CUP OR SPOON WITH NON-
STICK VEGETABLE SPRAY. THIS WAY THE
HONEY SLIPS FREELY OFF THE SPOON
OR OUT OF THE CUP, AVOIDING A
STICKY SITUATION.

HONEY-ROASTED ROOT VEGETABLE SALAD

Honey-roasted root vegetables end up all sticky, crisp and nutty-flavoured, and are serious comfort food. I have used the same recipe with non-root vegetables, such as pumpkin and cauliflower, which are both delicious roasted, and like the root vegetables these can be served either hot or cold.

350G BABY CARROTS, SCRUBBED AND TRIMMED

350G BABY TURNIPS, SCRUBBED AND TRIMMED

400G PARSNIPS, PEELED, TRIMMED AND QUARTERED LENGTHWAYS

350G SMALL YAMS

350G BABY BEETROOT, SCRUBBED AND TRIMMED

4–6 TABLESPOONS OLIVE OIL

2 TABLESPOONS LIQUID HONEY

SEA SALT AND FRESHLY GROUND BLACK PEPPER

1 Preheat oven to 200°C. Place carrots, turnips, parsnips and yams in an oven pan, and beetroot in another (beetroot needs to be roasted separately as it bleeds its colour onto the other vegetables).

2 Drizzle vegetables with olive oil and honey, season with salt and pepper and toss well. Roast for 30 minutes or until golden brown, tossing once during cooking.

3 To make the dressing, whisk honey, mustard, lemon juice and oil in a bowl to combine. Season with salt and pepper. Pour dressing over warm vegetables and toss.

serves 4 as a side dish

HONEY DRESSING

2 TABLESPOONS FLORAL HONEY

2 TABLESPOONS WHOLEGRAIN MUSTARD

JUICE OF 1 LEMON

1/4 CUP WALNUT OIL (OR EXTRA VIRGIN OLIVE OIL)

SEA SALT AND FRESHLY GROUND BLACK PEPPER

KIDNEY BEAN COTTAGE PIE

My kidney bean cottage pie is a vegetarian's delight – though you'll find many an unsuspecting meat-lover will fall for this potato-topped pie too.

PARMESAN POTATO TOPPING

800G FLOURY POTATOES (I USE AGRIA POTATOES), PEELED AND COOKED

50G BUTTER

½ CUP WARMED MILK

⅓ CUP FRESHLY GRATED PARMESAN

SEA SALT AND FRESHLY GROUND BLACK PEPPER

KIDNEY BEAN FILLING

3 TABLESPOONS OLIVE OIL

1 ONION, DICED

3 CLOVES GARLIC, CHOPPED

1 CARROT, PEELED AND FINELY DICED

2 STALKS CELERY, FINELY DICED

420G CAN RED KIDNEY BEANS, RINSED AND DRAINED

400G CAN CHOPPED TOMATOES

2 TABLESPOONS TOMATO PASTE

3 TABLESPOONS CHOPPED FRESH THYME

SEA SALT AND FRESHLY GROUND BLACK PEPPER

1 Mash potatoes while still hot, add butter and milk and beat until smooth and fluffy. Beat in Parmesan and season with salt and pepper to taste.

2 Heat a saucepan, add olive oil, onion, garlic, carrot and celery and cook over a medium-low heat for 10 minutes, stirring regularly, until softened but not coloured.

3 Add kidney beans, canned tomatoes and juice and tomato paste and simmer for 10 minutes until thick and reduced. Add thyme and season with salt and pepper to taste.

4 Preheat oven to 180°C. Divide bean mixture between 4 x 1½ to 2-cup capacity ramekins. Top each with mashed potato. Bake for 20 minutes or until golden brown.

serves 4

GOOD IDEA ...
FOR FLUFFY-TEXTURED AND LUMP-FREE MASHED POTATOES, USE A POTATO RICER OR MOULI TO PURÉE THE COOKED POTATOES. OR, I FIND SIEVING MASHED VEGETABLES WORKS WELL TO PRODUCE A DIVINELY SMOOTH TEXTURE.

LAMB & OLIVE PIES WITH SCONE CRUSTS

My favourite pastry topping is this scone crust because it is wonderfully soft and light and reminds me of dumplings or my mother's light-as-air scones. Plus its softness really complements the hearty lamb stew beneath.

700G LAMB SHOULDER STEAKS, TRIMMED OF SKIN AND EXCESS FAT

OLIVE OIL

1 ONION, DICED

3 CLOVES GARLIC, CHOPPED

1 CUP STUFFED GREEN OLIVES

1½ CUPS REDUCED BEEF STOCK (AVAILABLE FROM SUPERMARKETS IN VACUUM PACKS)

FINELY GRATED ZEST OF 1 LEMON

1 TEASPOON GROUND CINNAMON

2 TABLESPOONS CHOPPED FRESH MARJORAM OR OREGANO

SALT AND FRESHLY GROUND BLACK PEPPER

1 Cut lamb into 2cm cubes. Heat a frying pan with a little olive oil and brown meat in batches. Remove meat to one side. Add onion and garlic to the pan and cook for 5 minutes to soften. Return meat to the pan. Add olives and stock and bring to the boil.

2 Reduce heat, half cover the pan and gently simmer for 1½ hours. Stir in lemon zest, cinnamon and marjoram, and season with salt and pepper to taste. Remove to a bowl to cool.

3 Divide mixture to fill 4 x 1½ to 2-cup capacity ramekins.

SCONE CRUST

2 CUPS PLAIN FLOUR

3 TEASPOONS BAKING POWDER

½ TEASPOON SALT

50G BUTTER

1 CUP MILK

1 Combine flour, baking powder and salt in a bowl. Rub butter into flour by hand until crumbly. Stir in milk to bring together into a soft, smooth dough. Wrap in plastic wrap and refrigerate for 20 minutes before rolling out.

2 Roll out pastry to 4mm and cut to cover ramekins. Brush edges of ramekins with water and cover with pastry lids. Press edges with a fork to secure, and cut a hole in the centre of each lid to release steam during cooking. Refrigerate for 20 minutes. Preheat oven to 190°C.

3 Bake pies for 20–25 minutes or until crusts are puffed and golden brown.

BAKING TIP ...
WHEN RUBBING BUTTER INTO FLOUR, TAKE CARE NOT TO OVERWORK THE MIXTURE OR THE BUTTER WILL BECOME OILY AND THE PASTRY STICKY. IF USING A FOOD PROCESSOR, PULSE THE MIXTURE IN SHORT BURSTS.

serves 4

MUSHROOM & TOFU PIES

We all know that we need to eat at least five servings of fresh vegetables and fruit a day for good health. We can achieve this in a very tasty way by incorporating more vegetable-based meals into our life, whether we're vegetarian or not.

3 TABLESPOONS SUNFLOWER OIL
250G FIELD MUSHROOMS, THICKLY SLICED (RESERVE 4 SLICES FOR DECORATION)
250G BUTTON MUSHROOMS, HALVED
350G FIRM TOFU, CUT INTO 1CM CUBES
5 SPRING ONIONS, FINELY SLICED
PINCH CHILLI POWDER
3 TABLESPOONS LIGHT SOY SAUCE
2 TABLESPOONS HOISIN SAUCE
2 SHEETS READY-ROLLED PUFF PASTRY
1 EGG, LIGHTLY BEATEN WITH A LITTLE MILK TO GLAZE

1 Heat a large frying pan or wok and stir-fry mushrooms, tofu and spring onions in oil for 5–8 minutes or until lightly browned. Add chilli powder, soy and hoisin sauces and toss well over heat for a few minutes. Set aside to cool to room temperature.

2 Divide the cold mixture between 4 x 1½-cup capacity ramekins or pie dishes. Cut out pastry to form lids and place over filling. Secure edges by pressing with the tines of a fork. Cut several slits in the surface to allow steam to escape, and decorate each pie with a slice of mushroom. Chill for 30 minutes. Preheat oven to 210°C.

3 Brush pastry lids with egg glaze. Bake for 20–25 minutes until puffed and golden brown.

serves 4

MY ADVICE ...
DON'T STRETCH THE PASTRY WHEN TOPPING OR LINING PIE TINS – GENTLY EASE IT INTO PLACE. IF YOU FOLLOW THIS PROCEDURE, IT WILL PREVENT THE PASTRY SHRINKING DURING COOKING.

SPICY FISH & RICE STEW

I've tailored this recipe for busy weeknight preparation by reducing the cooking time and countering this by increasing aromatic seasonings, such as coriander, spices and lemon juice, to boost the taste sensation.

2 TABLESPOONS OLIVE OIL

1 RED ONION, FINELY DICED

2 TEASPOONS GARAM MASALA

400G CAN SWEETCORN KERNELS, DRAINED

400G CAN CHOPPED TOMATOES

2 CUPS CHICKEN STOCK

JUICE OF 3 LEMONS

1/2 CUP LONG GRAIN RICE

600G WHITE FISH FILLETS, CUT INTO 2CM CUBES

1/4 CUP CHOPPED FRESH CORIANDER

SEA SALT AND FRESHLY GROUND BLACK PEPPER

1 Heat a large saucepan, add oil and onion and cook over a medium heat for 5 minutes to soften but not colour. Add garam masala and cook for 1 minute.

2 Add sweetcorn, tomatoes, stock and lemon juice and simmer for 10 minutes.

3 Add rice and cook for 8 minutes, then add cubed fish and simmer for 5–7 minutes until rice is tender. Stir in coriander and season with salt and pepper to taste.

serves 4

GOOD IDEA …
THIS ONE-POT COOKING METHOD IS A CINCH AS ALL THE INGREDIENTS GO INTO A SINGLE VESSEL TO PRODUCE A COMPLETE MEAL. PLUS, THERE'S THE DELICIOUS ADDED BONUS OF MINIMAL WASHING-UP! THE POT CAN COOK OVER DIRECT HEAT ON THE STOVE-TOP OR IN THE OVEN, BUT THE KEY IS TO KEEP THE HEAT DOWN SO THAT THE FOOD SIMMERS AND THE FLAVOURS ARE GENTLY EXTRACTED.

CHIANTI & PORCINI RISOTTO

Good wine, like any quality ingredient, will enhance a dish and can transform the humblest meal into a fine feast.
So don't compromise flavour by adding mediocre wine to cooking.

30G DRIED PORCINI MUSHROOMS

1/2 CUP BOILING WATER

2 CUPS QUALITY CHICKEN STOCK

3 TABLESPOONS OLIVE OIL

1 RED ONION, FINELY DICED

3 CLOVES GARLIC, CRUSHED

1 1/2 CUPS ITALIAN RISOTTO RICE,
SUCH AS CARNAROLI, VIALONE NANO
OR ARBORIO

1 CUP CHIANTI

3 TABLESPOONS CHOPPED FRESH
OREGANO

SEA SALT AND FRESHLY GROUND
BLACK PEPPER

1 Place porcini in a small bowl, cover with 1/2 cup boiling water and leave to soften for 5 minutes. Place stock in a small saucepan and bring to the boil, then turn down heat to just simmer. Once the porcini have softened, remove them to one side and add the soaking liquid to the hot stock.

2 Heat a large heavy-based pan, add oil, then onion and garlic, and sweat over a low heat for 10 minutes to soften but not colour. Raise the heat a little and add risotto rice to toast but not brown, stirring continuously for 2 minutes.

3 Add half the wine and stir over a medium heat until reduced. Add remaining wine and stir until reduced. Add a ladleful of hot stock and stir until liquid is reduced and the mixture is nearly dry. Repeat adding stock until it is all absorbed and the rice is al dente and the finished risotto has a creamy consistency (this takes 15–20 minutes).

4 Stir in porcini mushrooms and chopped fresh oregano, and season risotto with salt and pepper to taste. Remove pan from the heat, cover and leave to steam for 5 minutes before serving.

serves 4

MUSTARD-CRUSTED FILLET OF BEEF WITH BEETROOT PURÉE

Here I give you the best way to cook a fillet of beef, which is truly low in effort and high in taste and visual effect. Be sure to seek out a quality wholegrain mustard, as this will make a world of difference to the flavour of the finished beef.

BEETROOT PURÉE

4 MEDIUM-SIZED BEETROOT, SCRUBBED

½ CUP LOW-FAT SOUR CREAM

SEA SALT AND FRESHLY GROUND BLACK PEPPER

1 Cook whole beetroot in a saucepan of boiling water for 35–45 minutes or until tender. Drain and refresh with cold water until cool enough to handle. Remove skins, which should simply slip off.

2 Roughly chop beetroot and place in the bowl of a food processor with the sour cream. Process to form a smooth paste. Season with salt and pepper to taste. Gently reheat in a saucepan if necessary to serve hot.

BEEF & MUSHROOMS

1KG EYE FILLET OF BEEF, AT ROOM TEMPERATURE, TRIMMED

SEA SALT AND FRESHLY GROUND BLACK PEPPER

OLIVE OIL

⅓ CUP WHOLEGRAIN MUSTARD

12 MEDIUM-SIZED FIELD MUSHROOMS

1 Preheat oven to 220°C. Season beef with salt and pepper. Heat a large frying pan with an ovenproof handle. Add a little oil and brown beef over high heat for 1–2 minutes on all sides.

2 With a palate knife, spread mustard evenly over beef. Place pan in the oven to roast beef for 20–25 minutes to cook to medium-rare.

3 Remove beef from oven, cover loosely with foil and leave to rest in a warm place for 10 minutes before thickly slicing to serve.

4 Place mushrooms on a baking sheet, drizzle with a little olive oil and season with salt and pepper. Roast for 10 minutes to serve hot with beef and beetroot purée.

SERVING SUGGESTION ... FOR A MORE CASUAL APPROACH, SKIP PLATING-UP INDIVIDUAL MEALS – INVEST IN SOME BIG WHITE SERVING PLATTERS AND LET EVERYONE HELP THEMSELVES FROM THESE.

serves 6

BACON & TOMATO CHOWDER

Soup can be a single course or a whole meal, either way you'll find soup one of the most versatile and satisfying dishes to cook and serve at home. I recommend serving crusty bread or toasted bagels with this soup.

2 TABLESPOONS OLIVE OIL

8 SLICES RINDLESS BACON, ROUGHLY CHOPPED

1 LARGE ONION, FINELY DICED

600G (ABOUT 3 LARGE) WAXY POTATOES, SUCH AS NADINE OR DRAGA

2 CUPS CHICKEN STOCK

400G CAN CHOPPED TOMATOES

2 TABLESPOONS TOMATO PASTE

2 TABLESPOONS CHOPPED OREGANO

SEA SALT AND FRESHLY GROUND BLACK PEPPER

1 Heat a large saucepan, add oil and bacon to lightly brown, then add onion and cook over a gentle heat until softened but not coloured. Peel potatoes and cut into 1cm cubes.

2 Add potatoes, stock, tomatoes and tomato paste to the pan and bring to the boil, then simmer for 15 minutes or until potatoes are cooked through.

3 Add oregano and season with salt and pepper to taste.

serves 6

MY ADVICE ...
BY FOLLOWING A FEW BASIC RULES, GOOD SOUPS ARE HIGHLY ACHIEVABLE. IMPORTANT SOUP RULES INCLUDE: USE FRESH INGREDIENTS (NOT TIRED OLD ONES FROM THE BOTTOM OF THE FRIDGE), AS THESE INCREASE THE TASTE AND GOODNESS OF SOUP; USE GOOD STOCK AS A FLAVOUR BASE; AND SIMMER RATHER THAN BOIL SOUPS TO GENTLY EXTRACT THE MOST FLAVOUR FROM INGREDIENTS.

SERVING SUGGESTION ...
I FIND THAT INTERESTING
ACCOMPANIMENTS REALLY ADD TO
THE APPEAL OF SOUP. FOR INSTANCE,
A TOASTED CHEESE SANDWICH OR
GRILLED CREAMY FETA ON TOAST
IS FANTASTIC WITH TOMATO-BASED
SOUPS. PITA BREAD BRUSHED WITH
OLIVE OIL AND BAKED UNTIL CRISP
IS GREAT TO DUNK INTO DENSE
VEGETABLE SOUPS. THEN THERE'S
ALWAYS CRUNCHY CROUTONS OR
DRIPPING HOT GARLIC BREAD; AND
SAVOURY SCONES ARE ESPECIALLY
GOOD TOO.

CUBAN BLACK BEAN SOUP

Thick soups are particularly gratifying and by their nature filling – this one will even satisfy your soul.

3 TABLESPOONS OLIVE OIL

1 ONION, DICED

3 CLOVES GARLIC, CHOPPED

1 GREEN PEPPER, SEEDS REMOVED, FINELY DICED

1 TABLESPOON GROUND CUMIN

1/2 TEASPOON EACH GROUND CORIANDER AND ALLSPICE

2 CUPS DRIED BLACK BEANS, SOAKED OVERNIGHT IN PLENTY OF COLD WATER

2 BAY LEAVES

2 LITRES VEGETABLE OR CHICKEN STOCK

1/2 CUP CHOPPED FRESH CORIANDER

JUICE OF 1 LIME

SEA SALT AND FRESHLY GROUND BLACK PEPPER

1/2 CUP SOUR CREAM

1 AVOCADO, FINELY DICED TO GARNISH

1   Heat a large saucepan, add oil, onion, garlic and diced green pepper and cook over a gentle heat until softened but not coloured. Add spices and cook for 1 minute to toast.

2   Add black beans, bay leaves and stock and bring to the boil, then turn down the heat to simmer for 1 hour or until beans are very tender. Remove the bay leaves.

3   Purée half the mixture, then return this purée to the saucepan along with the coriander, lime juice, and season with salt and pepper to taste.

4   Serve in bowls topped with a dollop of sour cream and some diced avocado.

serves 6

CHICKEN UDON NOODLE SOUP

Remember that good stock is an important foundation of soup. I enjoy making my own when I have the time, however, prepared stocks are a good standby. Purchased stocks may be quite salty, so adjust seasoning at the end of cooking to allow for this.

6 CUPS CHICKEN STOCK

2 TABLESPOONS MISO PASTE

3 TABLESPOONS FINELY GRATED FRESH GINGER

3–4 TABLESPOONS LIGHT SOY SAUCE

2 SKINLESS CHICKEN BREASTS, FINELY SLICED

150G OYSTER MUSHROOMS (OR BUTTON MUSHROOMS), SLICED

400G UDON NOODLES

¼ CUP ROUGHLY CHOPPED CORIANDER LEAVES

3 SPRING ONIONS, SLICED INTO FINE STRIPS

1 Place chicken stock in a large saucepan and bring to the boil. Add miso paste, ginger, soy sauce and chicken, and simmer for 3 minutes. Add mushrooms and udon noodles, and simmer for a further 3 minutes.

2 Skim off any froth that may come to the surface. Stir in coriander and serve immediately, garnished with sliced spring onion.

serves 4

TAKE STOCK …
IT IS POSSIBLE TO USE PLAIN WATER OR VEGETABLE
COOKING WATER INSTEAD OF STOCK BUT IT'S
HARDER TO BUILD A FLAVOUR BASE THIS WAY –
ADDING LOTS OF HERBS AND SPICES CAN WORK
TO COUNTER-BALANCE THIS.

CREAMY CELERIAC SOUP WITH TRUFFLE OIL

Soup is one of my favourite habitats for root vegetables. I adore my celeriac soup; it's as sumptuous and smooth as silk. Celeriac is available in the colder months of the year, and while it looks rather bumpy and ugly it has a flavour that is deliciously unique.

1 TABLESPOON BUTTER

1 TABLESPOON EXTRA VIRGIN OLIVE OIL

1 LARGE ONION, CHOPPED

4 CLOVES GARLIC, CHOPPED

500G CELERIAC, PEELED AND ROUGHLY CHOPPED

500G (ABOUT 3 LARGE) MASHING POTATOES, PEELED AND ROUGHLY CHOPPED

6 CUPS VEGETABLE OR CHICKEN STOCK OR WATER

½ CUP CREAM CHEESE

SEA SALT AND WHITE PEPPER

TRUFFLE OIL OR QUALITY EXTRA VIRGIN OLIVE OIL TO SERVE

BASIL LEAVES TO GARNISH

1 Heat a large saucepan, add butter and oil to melt, then onion and garlic and cook for 10 minutes over a gentle heat until softened but not coloured. Add celeriac, potatoes and stock or water and bring to the boil. Simmer until vegetables are tender.

2 Purée mixture in a blender or food processor – this may need to be done in several batches. Add a little cream cheese to each batch and blend until smooth.

3 Season well to taste with salt and white pepper. Gently reheat to serve hot but do not boil or the soup may split. Serve drizzled with truffle oil or olive oil if desired and garnish with a sprig of basil.

serves 6

SUBSTITUTE ...
WHEN CELERIAC IS NOT AVAILABLE, SUBSTITUTE NUTTY-TASTING JERUSALEM ARTICHOKES (ALSO A LIMITED SEASON), OR PARSNIPS (AVAILABLE ALL YEAR ROUND) FOR THE CELERIAC TO CREATE DIFFERENT VERSIONS OF THIS FAVOURITE SOUP. IF TRUFFLE OIL IS A BIT BEYOND YOU, THEN A DOLLOP OF BASIL PESTO, WHICH MELTS INVITINGLY INTO THIS CREAMY SOUP, IS JUST AS HEAVENLY.

GOOD IDEA …
ROOT VEGETABLES LEND THEMSELVES
BEAUTIFULLY TO PURÉES. BOIL OR
ROAST UNTIL TENDER YOUR CHOSEN
VEGETABLE SUCH AS BEETROOTS,
CARROTS OR PARSNIPS. BLEND TO
A SMOOTH PURÉE IN A FOOD
PROCESSOR WITH A LITTLE GARLIC,
IF DESIRED, AND LOTS OF EXTRA VIRGIN
OLIVE OIL. SEASON WITH SALT AND
PEPPER. SERVE HOT AS A SIDE DISH
OR COLD AS A DIP, SPREAD, SALAD
OR ANTIPASTO.

SPICED LAMB SHANKS & VEGETABLES COOKED IN CARROT JUICE

One of the remarkable features of root vegetable cookery is that it can encompass the entire range of cooking methods from boiling, steaming, baking, grilling and frying to braising and roasting. As an example in innovation, I've cooked these slow-braised lamb shanks in vibrantly spiced carrot juice – instead of stock, and scattered baby carrot and turnips around the meat to create a whole meal.

4 LAMB SHANKS

½ TEASPOON CHILLI POWDER

2 TEASPOONS EACH GROUND CUMIN, PAPRIKA AND CORIANDER

2 TABLESPOONS CORNFLOUR MIXED WITH ½ CUP COLD WATER

2 CUPS CARROT JUICE (AVAILABLE FROM SUPERMARKETS OR JUICE YOUR OWN)

250G BABY CARROTS, TRIMMED

250G BABY TURNIPS, TRIMMED

SEA SALT AND FRESHLY GROUND BLACK PEPPER

1 Preheat oven to 180°C. Place lamb shanks in a casserole dish to fit snugly. Combine spices and cornflour with carrot juice and pour over lamb shanks. Cover and bake for 2 hours.

2 Remove from oven, turn the shanks over and add carrots and turnips, and season with salt and pepper. Return to the oven, uncovered, and bake for a further 30 minutes.

3 Skim any excess oil from the surface of the sauce before serving.

serves 4

CHOCOLATE PARSNIP CAKE

Parsnips have an extremely high natural sugar content so they are perfect as the main player in this cake.

1½ CUPS SUNFLOWER OIL
1½ CUPS CASTER SUGAR
1 TEASPOON VANILLA EXTRACT
3 LARGE EGGS
2 CUPS FINELY GRATED PARSNIP
(ABOUT 2 LARGE PARSNIPS)
½ CUP CHOCOLATE CHIPS
1 CUP FLOUR
1 TEASPOON BAKING POWDER
1 TEASPOON BAKING SODA
½ CUP DUTCH PROCESS
COCOA POWDER
2 TEASPOONS CINNAMON

1 Preheat oven to 190°C (170°C fan bake). Grease a 22cm springform cake tin and dust with flour.

2 With an electric mixer, whisk oil, sugar, vanilla and eggs to form a creamy mixture. Stir in grated parsnip, chocolate chips and remaining dry ingredients sifted together.

3 Pour mixture into prepared cake tin and bake for 1 hour 20 minutes or until a skewer inserted comes out clean but still a little moist. Turn out on a wire rack to cool. Ice with sour chocolate frosting once cold.

serves 12

SOUR CHOCOLATE FROSTING

½ CUP DARK CHOCOLATE,
COARSELY CHOPPED
½ CUP SOUR CREAM

1 Melt chocolate in a bowl over a pan of simmering water or microwave in short bursts. Stir until smooth, then set aside to cool a little.

2 Stir in sour cream, then beat mixture with a wooden spoon until creamy. Spread over cake.

HOW TO …
PREPARE A CAKE TIN. LIGHTLY SPRAY THE BASE AND SIDES OF THE TIN WITH OIL OR BRUSH EVENLY WITH MELTED BUTTER. LIGHTLY DUST WITH FLOUR: TAP THE TIN ON A BENCH TO SETTLE FLOUR, THEN TIP OUT ANY EXCESS.

DUTCH PROCESS COCOA POWDER …
GOES THROUGH A SPECIAL PROCESS,
INVENTED BY A DUTCHMAN (HENCE THE
NAME), TO NEUTRALISE THE COCOA'S
NATURAL ACIDITY. THIS HEIGHTENS THE
COLOUR AND MELLOWS THE FLAVOUR
OF THE COCOA, GIVING A FAR SUPERIOR
RESULT. YOU WILL CERTAINLY NOTICE
THE DIFFERENCE WHEN YOU TASTE,
FOR EXAMPLE, MY FAVOURITE
VALRHONA DUTCH PROCESS COCOA.

SELF-SAUCING MOCHA PUDDINGS

For many of us the compelling combination of coffee and chocolate is the perfect way to round off a good meal.
These self-saucing mocha puddings go into the oven with the cocoa and coffee-flavoured liquid on top.
However, once cooked the chocolate sponge rises to the top, magically hiding a smooth dark chocolate sauce
few can resist.

125G BUTTER, SOFTENED

1/2 CUP CASTER SUGAR

2 EGGS

2/3 CUP SELF-RAISING FLOUR

PINCH SALT

2 TABLESPOONS DUTCH PROCESS
COCOA POWDER

1 Preheat oven to 190°C (170°C fan bake). Cream butter and sugar until pale, then beat in eggs. Fold in sifted dry ingredients.

2 Divide mixture between 4 individual 1 1/4 cup-capacity ovenproof dishes or ramekins.

3 Combine brown sugar, second measure of cocoa, coffee and boiling water and pour over pudding mix to evenly distribute between bowls. Bake for 35 minutes or until the sponge has risen and set. Serve hot with cream or ice-cream.

SAUCE

2/3 CUP BROWN SUGAR, TIGHTLY
PACKED

2 TABLESPOONS DUTCH PROCESS
COCOA POWDER

1 TABLESPOON INSTANT COFFEE

1 1/4 CUPS BOILING WATER

serves 4

COFFEE BEAN CHOCOLATE FUDGE CAKE

My coffee bean chocolate fudge cake recipe includes finely ground fresh coffee beans. Don't be alarmed at this addition. Rather than giving the cake a gritty texture, as some people fear, the ground beans simply contribute a more intense coffee taste. Any leftover cake keeps for up to a week in the fridge, so you can simply slice off slivers as necessary to relieve chocolate cravings.

125G BUTTER

125G DARK CHOCOLATE, COARSELY CHOPPED

1 CUP CASTER SUGAR

3 EGGS, BEATEN WITH A PINCH OF SALT

2 TABLESPOONS FINELY GROUND COFFEE BEANS

¼ CUP FLOUR, SIFTED

¼ CUP DUTCH PROCESS COCOA POWDER

MOCHA SAUCE TO SERVE (RECIPE BELOW)

1 Preheat oven to 190°C (170°C fan bake). Grease and lightly dust with flour a 22cm spring-form cake tin.

2 Melt butter and chocolate in a bowl over a saucepan of simmering water or microwave in short bursts. Stir until smooth, then set aside to cool slightly.

3 Stir sugar and then beaten eggs into cooled chocolate mixture. Quickly and gently stir in the ground coffee and then the sifted flour and cocoa. Pour mixture into prepared tin and bake for 40 minutes. The cake will be crisp on top but soft and still a little moist on the inside.

4 Leave to cool and firm in the tin before turning out. Cut into slivers to serve decorated with mocha sauce.

serves 10

MOCHA SAUCE

½ CUP ESPRESSO COFFEE

½ CUP DARK CHOCOLATE, ROUGHLY CHOPPED

1 Combine coffee and chocolate in a bowl and melt over a saucepan of simmering water, or microwave in short bursts. Stir until smooth.

makes 1½ cups

MY ADVICE ...
MELTING CHOCOLATE IS A DELICATE PROCESS – HIGH HEAT WILL CAUSE IT TO IRREVERSIBLY SEPARATE OR BURN. FOR BEST RESULTS, CHOP CHOCOLATE INTO SMALL PIECES BEFORE MELTING AS THIS ENSURES QUICK, EVEN MELTING AND AVOIDS LARGE LUMPS CATCHING AND BURNING. MELT CHOCOLATE IN A BOWL SET OVER GENTLY SIMMERING WATER, OR CAREFULLY MELT IN A MICROWAVE USING SHORT BURSTS AT A MEDIUM-LOW POWER LEVEL.

CINNAMON CHOCOLATE BABY CAKES

For the chocoholics out there, try these individually portioned cinnamon chocolate baby cakes blanketed with irresistibly glossy chocolate icing. I love how the complementary flavours of cinnamon and chocolate are woven together by this melt and combine method, which is almost ridiculously straightforward to prepare.

100G BUTTER
2 TABLESPOONS GOLDEN SYRUP
1 CUP CASTER SUGAR
1 CUP SOUR CREAM
1 EGG, LIGHTLY BEATEN
1¼ CUPS FLOUR
¼ CUP DUTCH PROCESS
COCOA POWDER
1 TABLESPOON CINNAMON
1 TEASPOON BAKING SODA
1 TEASPOON BAKING POWDER

1 Preheat oven to 190°C (170°C fan bake). Grease and lightly dust with flour 6 individual 1 cup-capacity cake or muffin pans.

2 Melt butter and golden syrup in a saucepan. Transfer to a bowl and add sugar, sour cream and egg, and beat until sugar has dissolved. Sift in the dry ingredients and gently stir to just combine.

3 Divide mixture between prepared pans and bake for 30 minutes or until cakes test cooked when a skewer inserted comes out clean.

4 Remove to a wire rack to cool. Once cold, drizzle with glossy chocolate icing.

makes 6

GLOSSY CHOCOLATE ICING

½ CUP CREAM
¾ CUP DARK CHOCOLATE MELTS
OR ROUGHLY CHOPPED DARK CHOCOLATE
1 TABLESPOON GOLDEN SYRUP

1 Place cream, chocolate and golden syrup in a bowl and melt over a saucepan of simmering water or microwave in short bursts. Stir to combine into a smooth icing.

MY ADVICE ...
I RECOMMEND USING PREMIUM DARK CHOCOLATE, WHICH MAY BE A LITTLE MORE EXPENSIVE BUT THE FLAVOUR DIFFERENCE IS IMMEASURABLE. MY ADVICE IS TO BUY THE BEST YOU CAN AFFORD – AS THE QUALITY INCREASES, SO WILL YOUR PLEASURE.

VALRHONA CHOCOLATE CARAMEL LOVE-HEART CAKES

Treat someone you love to a love-heart cake made with fine Valrhona chocolate.

100G BUTTER

200G VALRHONA CHOCOLATE, COARSELY CHOPPED

2 EGGS, LIGHTLY BEATEN

2/3 CUP SUGAR

1 TEASPOON VANILLA EXTRACT

1 CUP GROUND ALMONDS

2 TABLESPOONS DUTCH PROCESS COCOA POWDER, SIFTED

1 Preheat oven to 180°C (160°C fan bake). Grease and lightly dust with flour 8 x 150ml-capacity heart-shaped or round cake tins and line bases with non-stick baking paper, cut to fit.

2 Melt butter and chocolate together in a double boiler or microwave. Stir until smooth.

3 Whisk eggs, sugar and vanilla together until thick and pale. Fold the melted chocolate and butter into this mixture, then fold in the ground almonds and sifted cocoa to just combine.

4 Divide the mixture between the prepared cake tins. Bake for 20–25 minutes or until a skewer inserted comes out moist but clean. Cool for 15 minutes to set before removing from cake tins. Serve drizzled with equal quantities of glossy chocolate icing (see page 116) and caramel sauce.

CARAMEL SAUCE

100G SOFT CARAMEL SWEETS (I USE JERSEY CARAMELS), COARSELY CHOPPED

1/4 CUP CREAM

1 Place caramels in a saucepan with the cream and cook over a low heat for 5 minutes, stirring regularly until caramels melt into the cream to form a smooth sauce.

makes 8 small cakes

VALRHONA ...
GOES TO GREAT LENGTHS TO MAKE SUPERIOR QUALITY CHOCOLATE. FIRST THE HIGHEST QUALITY ESTATE-GROWN COCOA BEANS ARE CHOSEN, THEN ROASTED IN BATCHES FROM SEPARATE REGIONS AND ACCORDING TO VARIETY. THESE ARE FINELY GROUND AND CAREFULLY PROCESSED RESULTING IN CHOCOLATE THAT HAS A VELVETY TEXTURE AND INFINITE FLAVOUR ADVANTAGE.

CARROT CAKE MUFFINS

Paper-clad creations tied up with string are a striking way to present a simple muffin.

3 LARGE EGGS

1/2 CUP CASTER SUGAR

2 TABLESPOONS GOLDEN SYRUP

1/2 CUP SUNFLOWER OIL

1 CUP PLAIN YOGHURT

1 CUP (ABOUT 2 MEDIUM CARROTS) FINELY GRATED CARROT

2 CUPS SELF-RAISING FLOUR

1/2 TEASPOON BAKING SODA

1 TABLESPOON CINNAMON

5 BABY KIWIFRUIT, HALVED TO DECORATE

1 Preheat oven to 200°C (180°C fan bake). Cut 10 paper collars from non-stick baking paper measuring 10x20cm. Roll into cylinders and place in 10 1/2-cup capacity little cake tins or ramekins placed on a baking tray.

2 Combine eggs, sugar, golden syrup and oil in a mixing bowl and whisk until creamy. Stir in yoghurt and grated carrot.

3 Sift in dry ingredients and stir briefly until just combined. Spoon into prepared paper cylinders to 3/4 fill and bake for 20 minutes or until a skewer inserted comes out clean. Remove to a wire rack to cool.

4 Tie with twine and top with cream cheese icing and sliced baby kiwifruit, if desired.

makes 10

CREAM CHEESE ICING

125G CREAM CHEESE, AT ROOM TEMPERATURE

1/4 CUP CASTER SUGAR

FINELY GRATED ZEST AND JUICE OF 1 LEMON

1 Combine cream cheese and sugar in a bowl and beat until smooth. Add lemon zest and juice and beat to combine.

spring

WHEN SPRING ARRIVES, THE DAYS BEGIN TO LENGTHEN, AND PRODUCE RADIATES WITH UNRESTRAINED LIGHTNESS. TENDER LEAVES, CRISP ASPARAGUS SPEARS, PERFECT PEAS AND NEW POTATOES WILL ALWAYS TASTE BEST IN SPRING, THEIR NATURAL SEASON. THE FLAVOURS OF SPRING ARE AS FRESH AND VITAL AS THE SEASON — COOK AND EAT THEM WITH RENEWED RELISH.

CHAR-GRILLED ASPARAGUS WITH LEMON SAUCE

Asparagus responds well to a number of cooking methods, such as steaming, boiling, stir-frying, roasting, char-grilling and barbecuing. Each method results in a different taste and textural sensation. Char-grilling gives asparagus a definite burnt-nutty flavour that combines well with my lemon sauce, which is an easy and lighter version of that wickedly delicious French concoction, Hollandaise sauce.

400G FRESH ASPARAGUS, WOODY ENDS SNAPPED OFF

2 CLOVES GARLIC, CRUSHED

¼ CUP OLIVE OIL

SEA SALT AND FRESHLY GROUND BLACK PEPPER

1 Preheat a char-grill pan (or barbecue). Place asparagus spears in bowl with the garlic and olive oil and toss well. Season with salt and pepper and char-grill for 1–2 minutes on each side, turning once during cooking.

2 Serve asparagus hot as a starter with the lemon sauce on the side to dip.

LEMON SAUCE

100G BUTTER

JUICE OF 2 LEMONS

½ TEASPOON SALT

1 EGG YOLK

1 TABLESPOON MILK

1 Melt butter with the lemon juice and salt. Mix egg yolk with milk in a bowl, then pour melted butter and lemon onto yolks and whisk together.

2 Return mixture to the pan and heat very gently, whisking for 1 minute until sauce thickens. Do not boil or the sauce may curdle.

3 Serve asparagus as a starter with sauce on the side.

serves 4

MY ADVICE …
THE BEST WAY TO PREPARE ASPARAGUS IS TO
WASH THE SPEARS AND SNAP OFF THE TOUGH END
PORTIONS, RETAINING AS MUCH OF THE TENDER
GREEN SPEARS AS POSSIBLE. TO BE SURE TO
GAIN THE MAXIMUM NUTRITIONAL BENEFITS FROM
ASPARAGUS, ALWAYS COOK IT SOON AFTER PURCHASE.

HOW TO MAKE ...
HOME-MADE PESTO WITH
INCOMPARABLE TASTE AND TEXTURE:
COMBINE 2 BUNCHES OF SUMMER-
PICKED BASIL LEAVES (ABOUT 2 WELL-
PACKED CUPS), 2 CLOVES GARLIC,
1/4 CUP EACH PINE NUTS AND GRATED
PARMESAN IN THE BOWL OF A FOOD
PROCESSOR. PULSE TO CHOP. THEN,
WITH THE MOTOR RUNNING, DRIZZLE IN
1/2 CUP OLIVE OIL, BLENDING TO FORM
A SMOOTH PASTE. SEASON WITH SALT
AND PEPPER TO TASTE.

ASPARAGUS & PESTO TART

Home-made pesto will keep well stored in the fridge for up to 2 weeks. To keep it from discolouring, cover the surface with a thin film of olive oil.

OLIVE OIL TO GREASE TRAY
1 PRE-ROLLED SHEET PUFF PASTRY
1/4 CUP BASIL PESTO (RECIPE ABOVE)
20 MEDIUM-SIZED ASPARAGUS SPEARS
SEA SALT AND FRESHLY GROUND
BLACK PEPPER

1 Preheat oven to 220°C. Lightly grease an oven tray with oil or line with non-stick baking paper.

2 Lay puff pastry sheet on prepared tray. Score a 1cm frame around the edge of the pastry. Spread pesto to cover the pastry, avoiding the frame.

3 Trim asparagus to the same length as the pesto-covered central square of pastry and lay a row of asparagus spears on top of the pesto, alternating tip to end down the row. Season with salt and pepper.

4 Bake for 20 minutes or until pastry is puffed and golden and asparagus is tender. Remove to a large flat platter or board and slice to serve.

serves 4

ORZO, WATERCRESS & MARINATED ASPARAGUS SALAD

Orzo (sometimes called risoni) is a rice-shaped pasta that has a marvellous silken texture and a surprising ability to absorb other flavours, such as this vibrant watercress dressing.

1½ CUPS ORZO OR RISONI
(RICE-SHAPED PASTA)

1 BUNCH FINE PURPLE OR GREEN
ASPARAGUS SPEARS

¼ CUP EXTRA VIRGIN OLIVE OIL

SEA SALT AND FRESHLY GROUND
BLACK PEPPER

150G FETA, CRUMBLED

1 CUP WATERCRESS LEAVES,
PICKED FROM THE STEMS

1 Cook orzo in plenty of boiling salted water for 10–12 minutes or until tender to the bite. Drain, rinse in cold water and drain well.

2 Finely slice asparagus on an angle, discarding the woody ends of the spears. Place sliced asparagus in a bowl and combine with olive oil and season with salt and pepper. Leave to marinate for 30 minutes.

3 Combine cold orzo with the dressing and marinated asparagus and toss well. Mix in crumbled feta and watercress leaves. Adjust seasoning if necessary.

WATERCRESS DRESSING

4 CLOVES GARLIC, PEELED

1 CUP WATERCRESS, TIGHTLY PACKED

¼ CUP EXTRA VIRGIN OLIVE OIL

1 Place garlic and watercress in the bowl of a food processor and pulse to chop.

2 With the motor running, pour in oil slowly to form a smooth dressing. Season with salt and pepper to taste.

serves 4–6

GOOD IDEA ...
MANY PEOPLE DON'T REALISE THAT ASPARAGUS CAN ALSO BE EATEN RAW – IT'S BEST TO CHOOSE TENDER, THIN SPEARS FOR THIS PURPOSE. DICE, SLICE, OR SHAVE RAW ASPARAGUS AND ADD TO SALADS, OR MARINATE IN OLIVE OIL TO CREATE A CRUNCHY VEGETABLE TREAT AS I'VE DONE IN THIS ORZO SALAD.

SUBSTITUTE ...
A LOW-FAT OPTION IS TO REPLACE THE
CREAMY DIJON DRESSING WITH LOW-
FAT YOGHURT MIXED WITH A LITTLE
DIJON MUSTARD.

WARM NEW POTATO & SALMON SALAD

To ring the changes, use smoked chicken in place of the hot-smoked salmon and salmon roe in this warm potato and rocket combo.

800G NEW BABY POTATOES

400G HOT-SMOKED SALMON
(AVAILABLE FROM SUPERMARKETS)

2 CUPS ROCKET LEAVES

SEA SALT AND FRESHLY GROUND
BLACK PEPPER

100G SALMON ROE (OPTIONAL)

CREAMY DIJON DRESSING

2 EGG YOLKS

¼ TEASPOON SEA SALT

1–2 TEASPOONS DIJON MUSTARD,
TO TASTE

2 TABLESPOONS LEMON JUICE

½ CUP OLIVE OIL

1 Cook the potatoes in boiling salted water for about 10 minutes or until tender. Drain potatoes well, then quarter. Break up salmon into bite-sized pieces. Combine warm potatoes, salmon and rocket in a bowl. Season with freshly ground black pepper.

2 To make the dressing, place egg yolks, salt, mustard and lemon juice in the bowl of a food processor or blend in a bowl with a whisk or hand-held electric beater. Process or whisk until pale and foamy. With the motor running or while whisking constantly, add oil in a thin and steady stream until amalgamated.

3 Taste and adjust seasoning if necessary. Thin by whisking in a little hot water until desired consistency is reached. Drizzle dressing over salad ingredients and garnish with salmon roe if desired.

serves 4

HONEY CHILLI SQUID

I've included honey in this basic marinade as it gives the finished product a lovely caramel-like glaze and its sweetness counteracts the bite of garlic, the kick of chilli and the saltiness of soy sauce.

1KG LARGE SQUID TUBES, CLEANED AND HALVED
VEGETABLE OIL FOR FRYING
EXTRA SOY SAUCE TO SERVE

MARINADE

¼ CUP FISH SAUCE
3 TABLESPOONS LIQUID HONEY
3 CLOVES GARLIC, CRUSHED
2 SMALL RED CHILLIES, SEEDS REMOVED, FINELY CHOPPED

1 To make marinade, place fish sauce, honey, garlic and chillies in a bowl and whisk to combine. Set aside.

2 Score squid with the tip of a sharp knife, making a tight-knit criss-cross pattern on the inner side of each piece. Place in a non-metallic dish, pour marinade over squid, cover and refrigerate for 30–60 minutes.

3 Heat a wok or frying pan over a medium-high heat and stir-fry squid in several batches for 2–4 minutes – the honey will cause the squid to caramelise and can catch and burn, so keep it moving. Serve with extra soy sauce on the side.

serves 4

THIS GOES WITH THAT ... THIS MARINADE ALSO WORKS WELL WITH PRAWNS, SALMON STEAKS, CHICKEN BREASTS, PORK FILLET AND BEEF KEBABS.

PEA, PRAWN & NOODLE STIR-FRY

Peas are rich in natural sugars and I guess that's one reason why kids usually love this green vegetable so much.

300G EGG NOODLES

20 KING PRAWNS, PEELED LEAVING TAILS INTACT, DEVEINED

3 TABLESPOONS SESAME OIL

1 CUP SUGAR SNAP PEAS, TRIMMED

1 BUNCH SPRING ONIONS, ROUGHLY SLICED

1 CUP FRESHLY SHELLED PEAS

½ CUP BLUE PEA SPROUTS OR SUBSTITUTE MUNG BEAN SPROUTS

¼ CUP LIGHT SOY SAUCE

¼ CUP TAMARIND CONCENTRATE

1 Cook noodles in boiling salted water for 2–3 minutes or according to packet instructions until just tender. Drain well and set aside.

2 Meanwhile, heat a wok or large frying pan and stir-fry prawns in a little sesame oil for 2–3 minutes to cook. Remove to one side. Add vegetables to the pan and stir-fry with remaining sesame oil for 2–3 minutes.

3 Return prawns to the pan with the vegetables. Add the noodles, soy sauce (you may need to add more to taste) and tamarind, and toss well over high heat for 2–3 minutes or until liquid has reduced and all ingredients are hot. Serve immediately.

serves 4

CANTONESE COOKS … CONSIDER PEA SHOOTS, THE GROWING TIPS OF THE PLANT, A GREAT DELICACY. ALSO READILY AVAILABLE ARE SNOW PEA SPROUTS, WHICH ARE THIN WHITE STRANDS WITH CURLY PEA LEAFBUDS ON THE END; AND CRUNCHY NUTTY-TASTING BLUE PEA SPROUTS, WHICH I'VE USED HERE IN MY PEA AND PRAWN STIR-FRY.

SPRING PEA & MINT SOUP

When buying fresh peas, look for bright green waxy pods without any splits or bulges as these generally indicate the peas are past their prime. The season for fresh peas is short but as you know this vegetable is available frozen all year round.

SHORTCUT ...
IT'S GOOD TO KNOW THAT THE OPTION OF FROZEN PEAS IS A QUICK BUT EQUALLY HEALTHY ALTERNATIVE TO FRESH PEAS. THEY ARE SNAP FROZEN SHORTLY AFTER HARVEST SO THAT ALL THEIR GOODNESS IS PRESERVED. THIS RECIPE CAN BE MADE WITH FROZEN PEAS IF DESIRED.

3 TABLESPOONS OLIVE OIL

1 ONION, DICED

2 CLOVES GARLIC, CHOPPED

500G (2 LARGE) FLOURY POTATOES (I USE AGRIA POTATOES), PEELED AND DICED

4 CUPS CHICKEN STOCK

500G SHELLED PEAS

2 TABLESPOONS CHOPPED FRESH MINT

¼ CUP CREAM (OPTIONAL)

SEA SALT AND FRESHLY GROUND BLACK PEPPER

1   Heat oil in a large saucepan, add onion and garlic and cook over a medium heat for 5–10 minutes until softened but not coloured.

2   Add potatoes and chicken stock and bring to the boil, then simmer for 10 minutes until potatoes are soft. Add the peas and simmer for 5 minutes more. Add the mint and cream if desired.

3   Purée the mixture in a blender or food processor and season to taste with salt and pepper. Gently reheat soup to serve hot with crusty bread.

serves 4

BRUSCHETTA WITH RICOTTA & SMASHED PEA SPREAD

The sensation of eating fresh peas for the first time is an indelible childhood memory. First came the discovery of how to cleverly pop the irresistible little things into my mouth, straight from the burst pod, and then I remember being amazed that a garden vegetable could taste so sweet. This pea spread reminds me of the first fresh peas I ever tasted.

SLICED SOURDOUGH OR OTHER
RUSTIC BREAD

2 CLOVES GARLIC, PEELED AND
CUT IN HALF

EXTRA VIRGIN OLIVE OIL

½ CUP RICOTTA

1 To make the bruschetta, char-grill or toast the bread on both sides. Rub one side with garlic and brush with extra virgin olive oil.

SMASHED PEA SPREAD

1 CUP FRESHLY SHELLED PEAS, BLANCHED
IN BOILING WATER FOR 3 MINUTES

1 CLOVE GARLIC, PEELED

2 TABLESPOONS FRESHLY GRATED
PARMESAN

2 TABLESPOONS CHOPPED FRESH BASIL

2 TABLESPOONS EXTRA VIRGIN OLIVE OIL

SEA SALT AND FRESHLY GROUND
BLACK PEPPER

1 To make the spread, pound cold peas and garlic in a mortar and pestle or food processor until thick but still textural.

2 Stir in Parmesan, basil and olive oil, and season to taste with salt and pepper.

3 To serve, spread a layer of ricotta on bruschetta, then top with smashed pea spread.

makes 1 cup

BRUSCHETTA ...
(PRONOUNCED BROO-SKET-TA) REFERS TO SLICES OF CRUSTY BREAD
THAT ARE TOASTED THEN RUBBED WITH GARLIC AND DRIZZLED WITH
OLIVE OIL. THESE ITALIAN TOASTS ARE THE PERFECT BASE FOR MANY
DIFFERENT TOPPINGS AND SPREADS.

FRAGRANT BEEF SALAD WITH SPRING GREENS & RICE NOODLES

It's possible to rework this rice-noodle salad by substituting pork, chicken or tofu for the beef.

125G RICE VERMICELLI NOODLES,
SOAKED IN HOT WATER FOR 10 MINUTES

500G THICK BEEF RUMP OR SIRLOIN
STEAKS, TRIMMED OF EXCESS FAT

BUNCH SPRING ONIONS, FINELY SLICED

½ TELEGRAPH CUCUMBER, SEEDS
REMOVED, FINELY SLICED

200G GREEN BEANS, TRIMMED, HALVED
LENGTHWAYS, BLANCHED

½ CUP EACH CORIANDER AND
BASIL LEAVES

½ CUP VIETNAMESE MINT OR
ORDINARY MINT LEAVES

1. Drain noodles, then cook in a saucepan of boiling water for 1–3 minutes. Drain well, rinse in cold water, drain again and set aside to cool.

2. Heat a char-grill pan and brown meat over a high heat for 3–4 minutes on each side for medium-rare. Set beef aside to cool, then slice thinly.

3. Mix cold noodles, sliced beef and remaining salad ingredients in a bowl.

4. Combine dressing ingredients to taste, adding a little more of any particular ingredient to achieve a balanced taste. Pour dressing over salad and toss well.

serves 4

FRAGRANT DRESSING

1 TABLESPOON SESAME OIL

¼ CUP FISH SAUCE

¼ CUP FRESH LIME JUICE

¼ CUP SWEET CHILLI SAUCE

JENNIFER'S TOMATO TART

I want to encourage you to make my favourite tomato tart. This delicacy comes from the recipe collection of my good friend and talented chef, Jennifer Le Comte, who first tasted it while living in France. Jennifer and I worked together in Auckland for years and discovered that coincidentally we had worked overseas, at different times, for French women who were friends.

400G SHORT CRUST PASTRY

3 TABLESPOONS OLIVE OIL

1 ONION, FINELY CHOPPED

3 CLOVES GARLIC, CRUSHED

2 X 400G CANS ITALIAN TOMATOES, CHOPPED

4 LARGE EGGS

½ CUP CREAM

SEA SALT AND FRESHLY GROUND BLACK PEPPER

1 Roll out pastry to 3mm thick and use to line a 24cm deep-sided tart tin. Prick the base with a fork and chill for at least 30 minutes.

2 Heat a saucepan, add oil and onion, and cook over a moderate heat for 5 minutes to soften but not brown. Add garlic and tomatoes and simmer for 20 minutes, stirring regularly until the mixture thickens and nearly all the moisture has evaporated. Remove to one side to cool.

3 Preheat the oven to 220°C. Line the pastry case with baking paper or foil and fill with baking beans (I use chickpeas reserved for this purpose). Bake for 15 minutes, then remove the paper and beans and return the pastry case to the oven for a further 5 minutes to dry out. Reduce oven temperature to 160°C.

4 Combine eggs and cream with cooled tomato mixture and season well with salt and pepper. Pour this mixture into the baked pastry case and bake for 35–40 minutes or until just set.

serves 8

MY ADVICE ...
I ALWAYS HAVE A STOCK OF CANNED TOMATOES IN MY STORE CUPBOARD AS THIS VERSATILE STAPLE FORMS THE BASE OF ANY NUMBER OF TASTY MEALS. AND IT'S GOOD TO KNOW THAT CANNED TOMATOES ARE AS VIBRANT AS FRESH ONES – CHECKING THE LABEL REVEALS THERE'S NOTHING BUT TOMATOES AND THEIR JUICE IN THE CAN.

SPRING LAMB TIKA MASALA WITH CHICKPEA & TOMATO STEW

I find lamb racks are a real treat to cook. Conveniently prepared by the butcher, they look smart, taste succulent and lend themselves to all sorts of coatings. Tika Masala is a brilliantly aromatic Indian curry paste and is classically combined with chicken, but I find it works really well with lamb too. You will find it in jars or cans at the supermarket.

2 FRENCH-TRIMMED LAMB RACKS
(WITH 10 CUTLETS EACH),
AT ROOM TEMPERATURE
½ CUP TIKA MASALA PASTE
½ CUP THICK YOGHURT

1 Preheat oven to 220°C. Divide each lamb rack in 2, to make 4 portions with 5 cutlet bones each.

2 Combine Tika Masala paste and yoghurt in a bowl. Slather this mix over all surfaces of the lamb, taking care to leave the bones clean. Place racks in a lightly oiled oven pan and roast for 20 minutes for medium-rare.

3 Remove to rest and keep warm for 10 minutes before serving on top of portions of chickpea and tomato stew.

CHICKPEA & TOMATO STEW

3 TABLESPOONS OLIVE OIL
2 ONIONS, SLICED
3 CLOVES GARLIC, CHOPPED
2 X 400G CANS CHICKPEAS, RINSED
AND DRAINED
2 X 400G CANS DICED TOMATOES
SEA SALT AND FRESHLY GROUND
BLACK PEPPER
¼ CUP CHOPPED FRESH CORIANDER
OR MINT

1 Heat a saucepan, add oil and cook onions over a medium heat for 5–8 minutes until softened. Add garlic and cook for a few minutes more.

2 Add chickpeas and tomatoes and simmer for 5–8 minutes until thick and saucy. Season with salt and pepper to taste; stir in coriander or mint at the last minute.

serves 4

SERVING SUGGESTION . . .
I QUITE OFTEN SERVE THIS CHICKPEA AND TOMATO STEW AS A MEAL IN ITSELF AND FIND IT'S A GREAT OPTION FOR VEGETARIANS. TO UP THE VEGETABLE CONTENT OF THIS SOLO DISH, I STIR IN A FEW HANDFULS OF BABY SPINACH LEAVES AT THE LAST MINUTE SO THAT THEY JUST WILT, ADDING AN EXTRA VIBRANT SPLASH OF GREEN TO THE MIX.

GINGER PORK NOODLES

Ginger has a natural affinity with all meats, poultry and seafood and therefore works exceptionally well to boldly flavour this unpretentious pork dish.

400G PORK MINCE

4 TABLESPOONS DARK SOY SAUCE

2 TABLESPOONS PEANUT OIL

2 CLOVES GARLIC, CRUSHED

5CM PIECE FRESH GINGER, PEELED AND FINELY GRATED

1 TABLESPOON SESAME OIL

1 SMALL RED CHILLI, SEEDS REMOVED, FINELY CHOPPED

1 CUP CHICKEN STOCK

400G SHANGHAI OR HOKKIEN NOODLES

1 SMALL CUCUMBER, PEELED, SEEDED AND CUT INTO THIN STRIPS

1 Marinate the pork mince in soy sauce for 10 minutes. Heat a wok, add peanut oil, garlic, ginger and mince, and stir-fry for 5 minutes to brown. Add sesame oil, chilli and stock and simmer for 5 minutes.

2 Meanwhile, cook the noodles in a large pot of boiling water for 2 minutes, then drain well.

3 Arrange the hot noodles in bowls, ladle the sauce over and top with some cucumber strips. The contrasting textures of silky noodles, hot minced meat, and crisp cold cucumber are amazing.

serves 4

GOOD IDEA ...
WRAP PIECES OF PEELED GINGER ROOT TIGHTLY IN PLASTIC WRAP AND STORE IN THE FREEZER. WHEN GINGER IS REQUIRED IN A RECIPE, SIMPLY UNWRAP AND GRATE FROM FROZEN. THE BONUS TO THIS IS THAT FROZEN GINGER ROOT WILL GRATE CLEANLY WITHOUT ANY MASS OF MESSY FIBRES. RE-WRAP THE REMAINDER AND RETURN TO THE FREEZER TO HAVE ON HAND AT ALL TIMES; IT WILL LAST FROZEN FOR SEVERAL MONTHS.

HOW TO MAKE ...
A DIPPING SAUCE FOR THESE FISH
CAKES THAT CAN ALSO BE USED AS
A DRESSING FOR GRILLED FISH FILLETS
OR AS A MARINADE FOR MEAT SUCH AS
KEBABS OR STEAK: COMBINE EQUAL
QUANTITIES OF TAMARIND WATER, LIGHT
SOY SAUCE, THAI SWEET CHILLI SAUCE
AND CHOPPED FRESH CORIANDER IN A
BOWL AND MIX WELL.

TAMARIND FISH CAKES

Tamarind trees grow in tropical countries. However, the pulp of bean-like tamarind seedpods can be readily purchased from Asian and Indian speciality food stores.

500G WHITE FISH, BONED AND CUBED

3 CLOVES GARLIC, CRUSHED

3CM PIECE FRESH GINGER,
FINELY GRATED

2 SMALL GREEN CHILLIES, SEEDS
REMOVED, FINELY CHOPPED

¼ CUP TAMARIND WATER

1 EGG WHITE

½ CUP GROUND TOASTED PEANUTS

¼ CUP CHOPPED FRESH CORIANDER

SEA SALT TO TASTE

PEANUT OIL FOR FRYING

FRESH LIME WEDGES TO SERVE

1 Place the cubed fish in the bowl of a food processor and pulse to chop. Add garlic, ginger, chillies, tamarind water and egg white, and pulse until a chunky paste is formed. Add ground toasted peanuts, coriander and salt to taste, and pulse to just combine.

2 With damp hands, shape small portions of mixture into little cakes. Heat a frying pan and shallow-fry fish cakes in batches in hot peanut oil for 1–2 minutes on each side. Drain on paper towels. Take care not to overcook the fish cakes so that they remain moist.

3 Serve with fresh lime wedges and tamarind dipping sauce (recipe above) on the side to dip.

makes 24 small
fish cakes

TAMARIND CHICKEN WITH CASHEWS

Tamarind has a strange almost prune-like fragrance. It has a fabulous astringent-sour flavour, so is often used in place of lemon juice. Some recipes may call for the addition of a dash of honey, or brown or palm sugar, to balance the tang of tamarind, as in the following dish.

VEGETABLE OIL FOR FRYING, SUCH
AS SUNFLOWER SEED OIL

4 SKINLESS CHICKEN BREASTS

1 CUP TAMARIND CONCENTRATE

2CM PIECE FRESH GINGER,
FINELY GRATED

1/4 TEASPOON CHILLI POWDER

1/4 CUP LIQUID HONEY

3-4 TABLESPOONS LIGHT SOY SAUCE

1/4 CUP COLD WATER

1/2 CUP TOASTED CASHEW NUTS

CHOPPED FRESH CORIANDER TO GARNISH

1 Preheat oven to 180°C. Heat a frying pan, add a little oil and brown chicken breasts for 1–2 minutes on each side. Transfer to an oven pan.

2 Combine tamarind concentrate, ginger, chilli, honey and soy sauce to taste with 1/4 cup cold water, and pour this over the chicken. Place in oven to roast for 20 minutes or until chicken is just cooked through.

3 Slice each chicken breast into three to serve, spoon over sauce and scatter with cashew nuts and coriander to garnish.

serves 4

PRESERVED TAMARIND ...
COMES IN CONCENTRATED LIQUID OR COMPRESSED BLOCK FORMS.
THE CONCENTRATE CAN BE USED AS IS OR THINNED DOWN FURTHER
WITH THE ADDITION OF A LITTLE WATER. THE COMPRESSED BLOCKS
NEED SOAKING BEFORE USE. SIMPLY COVER BLOCKS WITH BOILING
WATER, WORK PULP INTO A PASTE WITH A FORK OR POTATO MASHER
(I FIND THE LATTER WORKS REALLY WELL) AND LEAVE TO SOAK FOR AT
LEAST 30 MINUTES. NEXT, STRAIN OFF THE LIQUID (THIS IS WHAT YOU
WANT) AND DISCARD THE SEED PULP, AS IT IS INEDIBLE. THE RESULTING
LIQUID IS SOMETIMES CALLED 'TAMARIND WATER' IN RECIPES. STORE
PREPARED TAMARIND WATER IN THE REFRIGERATOR SO THAT IT IS
READY WHEN YOU NEED IT FOR COOKING (IT WILL LAST LIKE THIS FOR
2-3 WEEKS).

RHUBARB & VANILLA MERINGUE PUDDINGS.

My rhubarb and vanilla meringue puddings are guaranteed crowd-pleasers and offer a cosy way to end a spring dinner party.

1 BUNCH (600G) RHUBARB,
TRIMMED AND WASHED
1 VANILLA BEAN, SPLIT IN HALF
LENGTHWAYS
1/4 CUP WATER
1/2 CUP SUGAR

MERINGUE TOPPING

3 EGG WHITES
1 TEASPOON VANILLA EXTRACT
1 CUP CASTER SUGAR

1 Cut rhubarb into 2cm lengths and place in a saucepan with the vanilla bean and 1/4 cup water. Cover pan and cook rhubarb over a low heat for 8 minutes. Remove vanilla bean and add sugar and stir until dissolved. Divide between 6 ramekins. Preheat the oven to 200°C.

2 To make the meringue, place egg whites in a clean bowl and whisk with an electric beater until soft peaks form. Add the vanilla extract, then gradually add the sugar while continuing to whisk for a few minutes until the mixture is thick and glossy.

3 Spread meringue evenly over the tops of the rhubarb making sure it reaches the edges of each ramekin.

4 Bake for 5 minutes until tips of meringue are golden. Serve warm with whipped cream on the side if desired.

serves 6

BAKING TIP ...
EXCESS EGG WHITES CAN BE STORED FOR FUTURE USE BY FREEZING IN PLASTIC BOTTLES FOR UP TO 6 MONTHS. BRING THEM TO ROOM TEMPERATURE BEFORE USING IN BAKING. TO CONVERT BULK EGG WHITES FOR USE IN RECIPES: 30MLS IS EQUIVALENT TO 1 EGG WHITE.

RHUBARB ...
IS IN SEASON FROM LATE WINTER/EARLY
SPRING ... THOUGH WITH MODERN
GROWING METHODS, RHUBARB IS NOW
AVAILABLE ALL YEAR ROUND.

COCONUT & RHUBARB PUDDINGS

The tartness of rhubarb creates an appealing contrast to the sweetness of these fragrant coconut puddings.

125G BUTTER, SOFTENED
½ CUP CASTER SUGAR
2 SMALL EGGS
1 CUP DESICCATED COCONUT
½ CUP SELF-RAISING FLOUR

RHUBARB TOPPING

1 CUP WATER
JUICE OF 1 LEMON
¼ CUP SUGAR
6 STALKS RHUBARB, CUT INTO
5CM LENGTHS

1 Preheat oven to fan bake 175°C. Cream butter and sugar, add eggs and beat well. Stir in coconut and flour to form a paste. Spoon into 4 small ovenproof bowls. Bake for 25 minutes or until a skewer inserted comes out clean.

2 Meanwhile prepare the rhubarb topping by placing the water, lemon juice and sugar in a saucepan. Bring to the boil, then turn down the heat to simmer for 2–3 minutes. Add the rhubarb to gently poach for a few minutes until just tender but still holding its shape.

3 Remove puddings from oven. Arrange some rhubarb on top of each and drizzle with some syrup. These puddings can be made 1–2 days in advance.

serves 4

CRANBERRY CUPCAKES WITH TEA INFUSION SYRUP

With these heavenly syrup-drenched cupcakes, I offer you a completely different way to enjoy afternoon tea.

CRANBERRY CUPCAKES

125G BUTTER, SOFTENED
¾ CUP CASTER SUGAR
FINELY GRATED ZEST OF 1 LEMON
3 EGGS
½ CUP THICK PLAIN YOGHURT
1 CUP PLAIN FLOUR
1 TEASPOON BAKING POWDER
¾ CUP DRIED CRANBERRIES (CRAISINS)

1 Preheat oven to fan bake 160°C. Grease and flour 12 180ml-capacity muffin pans.

2 Combine butter and sugar in a bowl and beat until pale and creamy. Beat in zest, eggs and yoghurt. Fold in sifted dry ingredients and cranberries. Spoon into prepared muffin pans.

3 Bake for 20 minutes or until a skewer inserted comes out clean. Turn out onto a wire rack to cool completely. Pour hot syrup over cold cakes.

TEA INFUSION SYRUP

4 HERBAL INFUSION TEABAGS
(I USE CRANBERRY, RASPBERRY AND ELDERFLOWER TEA)
2 CUPS BOILING WATER
1 CUP SUGAR
JUICE OF 2 LEMONS

1 Infuse teabags in boiling water for 10 minutes, then strain the liquid into a saucepan. Add remaining ingredients and bring to the boil, stirring until sugar dissolves. Boil for 5 minutes to form a syrup.

makes 12

MY ADVICE ...
OXYGEN DRAWS THE FLAVOUR OUT OF TEA LEAVES. SO, WHEN MAKING TEA, ALWAYS FILL THE KETTLE WITH FRESH COLD WATER AND DO NOT OVER-BOIL – THIS WILL MAKE THE MOST OF THE WATER'S OXYGEN CONTENT AND GIVE A CLEAN, BRIGHT-FLAVOURED BREW.

LIME DELICIOUS

Lime delicious is a classic self-saucing sponge pudding, made divinely fragrant with a good grating of lime zest.

25G BUTTER, SOFTENED
½ CUP SUGAR
FINELY GRATED ZEST OF 2 LIMES
JUICE OF 4 LIMES
2 EGGS, SEPARATED
150MLS MILK
3 TABLESPOONS FLOUR
ICING SUGAR TO DUST

1 Preheat oven to 180°C (160°C fan bake). Grease 6 x 180ml-capacity ramekins.

2 Place butter and sugar in a bowl and beat until pale and creamy. Whisk in lime zest and juice, egg yolks and milk, and fold in flour. Whisk egg whites to soft peaks and carefully fold into first mixture.

3 Spoon into prepared ramekins and bake for 15–20 minutes until puffed and golden. Remove from oven, dust with icing sugar and serve immediately because these soufflé-like puddings will quickly deflate.

serves 6

ZEST …
IS THE COLOURED OUTER RIND OF CITRUS FRUITS (MINUS THE WHITE PITH). THE ZEST IS PARTICULARLY POTENT AND CAN BE GRATED, PEELED IN STRIPS OR SHREDDED OFF WITH A GADGET CALLED A ZESTER. THE ZEST CONTAINS ESSENTIAL CITRUS OILS AND IS THEREFORE VERY FRAGRANT, SO USE THIS WHEN YOU WANT TO ADD AN EXTRA STRONG CITRUS ZING TO DESSERTS AND BAKING.

BAKED LEMON CUSTARDS

There's something addictive about the silky sweetness of this custard tinged with the tang of citrus that I find irresistible. I've tarted-up these custards with an adornment of candied lemon slices.

CANDIED LEMON SLICES

1 LEMON, FINELY SLICED
¼ CUP SUGAR
1 CUP COLD WATER

CUSTARD

4 SMALL EGGS
¾ CUP CASTER SUGAR
JUICE OF 3 LEMONS
¾ CUP CREAM

1. Preheat oven to 150°C. To make the topping, place sliced lemons, sugar and water in a saucepan and bring to the boil. Simmer for about 15–20 minutes until liquid is reduced and syrupy, and lemon slices are candied.

2. To make the custard, place all ingredients in a bowl and whisk to combine. Pour mixture into 6 x 180ml-capacity ramekins. Place ramekins in an oven pan and pour hot water into the pan to come half way up the sides of the ramekins. Bake for 20–25 minutes until just set but still a little wobbly in the centre.

3. Remove to cool, then refrigerate to chill a little before serving. Place one slice of candied lemon on top of each custard before serving.

serves 6

MY ADVICE...
SQUEEZE EXCESS LEMONS FOR THEIR JUICE AND FREEZE THIS FOR LATER USE. A GOOD IDEA IS TO FREEZE JUICE IN ICE-CUBE TRAYS, THEN THE FREE-FLOW JUICE-CUBES CAN BE DEFROSTED AS NEEDED OR, FOR EXAMPLE, DROPPED DIRECTLY INTO HOT SAUCES TO MELT.